a WRITERS CEILIDH for NEIL GUNN

a WRITERS CEILIDH for NEIL GUNN

George Mackay Brown

Donald Campbell

Robert Alan Jamieson

Robin Jenkins

Jessie Kesson

Norman Malcolm MacDonald

Aonghas MacNeacail

Naomi Mitchison

Bess Ross

Iain Crichton Smith

illustrated by Simon Fraser

edited by Aonghas MacNeacail

BALNAIN BOOKS

Printed by BPCC Wheatons, Exeter
Cover printed by Wood Westworth.
Published in 1991
by Balnain Books
Druim House, Lochloy Road, Nairn IV12 5LF

The publisher would like to acknowledge with gratitude
the financial assistance of:
    HI-Light (a part of Highlands and Islands Enterprise)HI-LIGHT

The Scottish Arts Council

British Library Cataloguing-in-Pulication Data:
A writers ceilidh for Neil Gunn
    I. Brown, George Mackay. 1921-
    II. MacNeacail, Aonghas III. Gunn, Neil M. (Neil
    Miller), 1891-1973
    820.800914

ISBN 1-872557-11-2

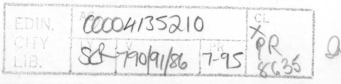

CONTENTS

Introduction   Aonghas MacNeacail   9

The Voyage of the Flood-Tide George Mackay Brown 35

The Campaign against Blonc   Naomi Mitchison 59

Cold in Coventry   Jessie Kesson 99

The Shutter Falls   Norman Malcolm MacDonald 113

The Greengrocer and the Hero   Robin Jenkins 125

The Cutting-Off Piece   Donald Campbell 159

The Last Black Hoose   Robert Alan Jamieson 195

Bun, Geugan, Duilleag / Roots,
Branches, Leaves   Aonghas MacNeacail 211

The Big Boat   Bess Ross 235

The Red Coffin   Iain Crichton Smith 247

ACKNOWLEDGEMENTS

A shared interest in Neil Gunn, and the themes which preoccupied him, drew the editor and illustrator into a collaboration which became the Balnain imprint's first publication. It is therefore appropriate that their professional acquaintance is renewed on this project, which at the enthusiastic instigation by Kate Martin of *HI-Light* (a part of the Highlands & Islands Enterprise) pays homage to Gunn himself and his achievements.

Acknowledgements for background information on the writers represented in this volume are due to the authors of various critical and historical studies. These include *The MacMillan Companion to Scottish Literature*, Ed. Trevor Royle (MacMillan); *The Literature of Scotland*, Roderick Watson (MacMillan); *The Scottish Novel*, F R Hart (Harvard); *A History of Scottish Literature*, Ed. Cairns Craig (Aberdeen University Press); *Contemporary Scottish Poetry*, Robin Fulton (MacDonald Publishers, Loanhead); *The Scottish Tradition in Literature* Kurt Wittig (Mercat Press). Particular thanks to the writers whose contributions have made this tribute possible.

⁻INTRODUCTION
Aonghas
MacNeacail

HIS BOOK IS OFFERED AS A tribute to Neil Miller Gunn, novelist, of Dunbeath, Caithness, in commemoration of the centenary of his birth. It celebrates him especially as a child of that greater part of Scotland popularly known as the 'Highlands and Islands.'

Topographically, and culturally diverse, the area nevertheless retains a distinctive identity of its own. Even at its least mountainous, it is never the 'Lowlands'. Many may regard it as peripheral, but it is not a 'Border' country. An Orcadian in the cities will have more in common with a native of Islay or Newtonmore than with one who grew up in the city.

The Highlands and Islands sustain at least four native languages of considerable pedigree. Gaelic was spoken all the way from Cape Wrath to the Mull of Kintyre, until fairly recently. There may be one or two surviving local Gaels in the East Sutherland fishing villages. The last known Perthshire Gael died this year. It's not so long since the last native speaker of

Aberdeenshire Gaelic died, and of course, there's evidence of the language right across the map of Scotland.

Scots, the language which replaced Gaelic as that spoken in the Scottish Court, in the days before Jamie the Saxt headed south to metamorphose into James the First, is today the language of the hearth in much of Caithness. It can be heard along the Moray coast, and in Perthshire. The use of Scots also has a considerable history in Kintyre, arising from contacts between local fishermen and their Ayrshire counterparts.

Further north, Shetlandic Norn has a particular cachet of its own. Modern Shetlandic is, in the words of poet and novelist Robert Alan Jamieson, 'an uneasy combination of English, Lowland Scots and Norrœna, or Norn, which was the language spoken in the isalnds from their settlement by the Norsemen... until well into the eighteenth century'.

Highlanders who had access to none of the indigenous languages, and many who did, have also frequently demonstrated considerable accomplishment in the Imperial language, Standard English. From such as the itinerant Martin Martin, Adam Ferguson — Perthshire Gael, and founder of the Social Sciences — and Thomas Urquhart of Cromartie — first to undertake the gargantuan task of translating Rabelais — to those represented in this anthology, the region has produced an unusual proportion of adepts in the English language. Not least among such artists was the man to whom the works collected here

INTRODUCTION

are dedicated, Neil Gunn himself.

Gunn, of course, as an excise officer, had many opportunities to travel throughout the region. Although not a Gaelic speaker, he was only a generation away from direct contact with a rich Gaelic heritage of story, song and lore. More than enough of it survived in local tradition to suffuse his fiction. His surname connects him with a Northern culture, another language, with an epic literature of its own. This also brought its many nuances, heroic, tragic, optimistic, into the store of resources available to his imagination.

On the other side of the world, as he was to discover, there existed a culture of complexities and simplicities which resonated in many ways with his own. Zen, he perceived, would not be out of place in the glen. Japan may have retained more of its direct links with the past. Gunn believed, with some justification, that enough of our older past survived to be able to reconstruct a similar Gaelic route to harmony.

This book, however, is not *about* Neil Gunn. It is not intended to be a work of hagiography or criticism. The objective is, rather, to present a sample of the imaginative vigour of contemporary Highland and Island writers, their creative diversity, and continuing commitment to explore the social, historical and philosophical concerns which animate the society they belong to. This seems a most effective way to honour the memory of one of our greatest novelists, who so manifestly shared those attributes and values.

The nature of society in the Highlands and Islands is, as elsewhere in the modern world, anything but homogenous. The crofter and the fisherman may have the highest profile in what is essentially, a rural demography, in a largely unfertile topography. Between the mountain, the peat moor and the skerry, they have built their shelters, and etched their delicately rendered livelihoods — ditch and lazybed — on that inhospitable landscape. But there are other features in the scene, equally human-inspired, and every bit as traditional to the area.

Even when it has been transformed into a Hotel, or Outdoor Centre, the 'Big House' is an unmistakable, and usually inescapable, presence in the Highland landscape. It may sit in splendid isolation, cut off from any sense of immediate community, or it may occupy a position of domination, which cannot be repudiated by its attendant village or town. It will have a history, which may only occassionally overlap with its surroundings, and then seldom benignly. It may cast a dark shadow. But not always.

There is the town itself. Every sizeable island, or district, needs its market place, where it can sell, or buy. More often the latter. Every market needs its infrastructure. Those who prepare, those who collect, those who deliver, and those who can clean up afterward, are the most essential, and usually unsung layer, without which the market could not function. Then there are those who agree the transaction, and those who witness. Healers will be required, physical and spiritual. Guidance and instruction may be re-

quired, to ensure that those who serve acquire the necessary skills. At this stage, matters become complicated. It becomes necessary to elect a Council, to ensure that such demands are effectively managed. Those who have experience in transactions make good Councillors. Local government reorganisation has not affected the latter principle.

Then there are the tourists. From the Haakons, Olafs, Sweyns and others, who came on their turbulent cruises and sometimes settled, through the Pennants and Boswell and Johnsons and the rest, who brought their diaries, to the blue-rinsed busloads of today — who sometimes settle — the traveller has always been part of Highland and Island life. As often as not, though, the traveller has been a Highlander, or Islander, returning for a brief visit to what will always be 'home', even if never returned to for more than a brief visit. And Highlanders and Islanders can themselves also be travellers for the sake of travelling.

Choosing the writers who could represent such a diversity within the confines of this book was actually fairly straightforward. There were only two specific criteria. Each writer should acknowledge the achievements of Gunn as one of the leading novelists of his time. They themselves should have connections, by birth, ancestry, or residence, with the Highlands and Islands.

The brief given to each writer was also simple, if unusual. 'Submit a piece of original work which can be presented as a gift to the memory of Neil Gunn.' They were not asked for recollections of the man

himself, nor for appraisals of his work. The contributions did not have to be in the style of Gunn, nor to dwell on themes which specifically concerned him. The writers were not asked to acknowledge his influence on the pieces they submitted. Nor, of course, were they asked to deny such an influence. Given a sense of shared environment, it would have been surprising if there had not been a recurrence of motifs — and motives — for which resonances could be found in his works.

Seniority is not the reason why George Mackay Brown's work leads this festival procession of words. He is there out of a more democratic concern for context. His story being in a sense, both a history and a metaphor, refers us both to Gunn and to a kind of creative background for all the other works presented.

Brown is a poet and novelist, steeped in the landscape of his native Orkney, and in a recurring symbolism deriving from the Catholicism to which he converted some thirty years ago. There is a chiselled feel to his language and imagery, which is wholly of the North. The quality found in even his most sensuous work is more that of an intensely-coloured jewel than the rich velvet and brocade qualities we normally associate with his chosen faith.

The story he gives us here, a subtly ludic *Voyage of the Flood-Tide*, is set, like so much of his work, in an undefined yet solidly rooted past. While it recreates and inhabits its own time, the story cleverly presages,

INTRODUCTION

in its fictionally renowned story-teller, Njal Gunnison of Dunbeath, that later weaver of tales who shares a birthplace with his imagined ancestor.

We are also at the beginning of an interweaving of Nordic and Celtic cultures, which has a continuing impact on life in the Highlands and Islands today. From Dingwall to Duirinish to Dell, from that macaronic Borgadelmore, in Kintyre, to Muckle Flugga, even in the most Gaelic of districts, Norse culture leaves its distinctive traces on our topography.

In the bone-structure of a face from the aforementioned Dell, in the Lewis Gaelic 'heartland', you'll see the features recognizable from the shores of the Skaggerak. The words you hear spoken may be in a Celtic language, but the tune in which they are uttered will be Scandinavian. That's several hundred years after the last Viking was supposedly driven out of the Western Isles. They never left. They are, in fact, in all of us; in the Gunns, the MacLeods, MacAulays, the Nicolsons and MacNicols — even in the lordly Macdonalds.

Both Viking and Gael had their honoured bards, and poetry of great quality. They had their stories and story-tellers, vivid shapers of lives and events, skilful builders of imagined landscapes. Ultimately, only the rhythms differ, and the shapes of the words.

Despite the Gaelic central element in his name, George Mackay Brown is a true child of the North. In *Voyage of the Flood-Tide*, as always, he invests a poet's sensibilities in the world he creates — a real,

three-dimensional world, rich with the complexities and simplicities of the real world we ordinarily inhabit. His distillation leaves an echo in our minds, a characteristic magical resonance. It is a reminder that the telling, and hearing, of tales and poems is as important to the health of the pschye as bread is to the gut.

Naomi Mitchison is the oldest contributor to this book, and indeed, one of Neil Gunn's oldest surviving friends. Their personal acquaintance began with a letter from Mrs Mitchison in 1940, in response to the publication of his novel *Second Sight*, which was not generally acclaimed. She also had reservations to express. Their correspondence continued for many years, during which they became, and remained firm friends.

Any disagreements they may have had, on matters which concerned one or other (contrary stands on the question of the individulal and the collective was one such issue), were far outweighed by the interests they shared. Society might have kept them well apart. He was the son of a Caithness crofter-fisherman, she the daughter of one of the great families of Perthshire, the Haldanes of Gleneagles. Her father, J.S. and brother J.B.S. were eminent in the sciences. Politics (of a leftist stream) and literature gave Neil and Naomi common ground.

Since her first work, *The Conquered*, a novel set among the Celts of ancient Gaul, was published in 1923, Naomi Mitchison has produced over seventy books including sixteen novels. Her settings range

INTRODUCTION

from Stone-Age Orkney through ancient Sparta, archaic Scythia, Imperial Rome to Outer Space. Her most local novel, *The Bull Calves*, described by Kurt Wittig as 'a serious attempt to recreate history as the people then must have seen it', is focussed on the family life of a fictional ancestor, Kirsty Haldane, in that disordered period immediately after Culloden.

In her note to this novel, she speaks of the need for 'mythologies which will be potent and protecting for our own era... for the individual, but also as social glue'. *Return to the Fairy Hill* (1966) is an account of her involvement with the Bakgatla people of Botswana. There she refers to a search for 'the open secret that we all know and which binds all life together. The sense of continuity between past and present. The stream of life which makes the individual both more and less important.' These are lodestones which Gunn would surely have recognised.

Her contribution to this anthology, *The Campaign against Blonc*, engages in its own subtle contemporary mythmaking. Blonc may be quite simply a big friendly, over-exuberant perhaps, family dog with a French name; he also seems to represent to the child narrotor something which is alien, mildly bestial. He may do daft things, but he does bring with his larger-than-life lolloping conduct an element of threat. He is cast in the role of Gorgon, until upstaged − violently − by a ram.

A childhood is evoked in this story which should be recognized as quintessentially Highland in its time

— even if not perceived as such by the great majority of Highlanders. Whether the setting is the author's native Perthshire or not, it could be, just as it could be Wiltshire, Wester Ross or East Sutherland. For this is the world of the 'Big House', with its Nurse and Mrs Cook and Simon the Butler and Jane the Parlour-Maid and visiting Bishops.

There is trouble on the North-West Frontier, and adults are overheard discussing Votes for Women, favourably, we may assume. By the end of the story, Blonc is defeated. 'The Tyranny is over', says the narrator, and 'I like these words. I chose them myself.' Perhaps this is not such a typical Big House after all. She remains wide-eyed and innocent, but has caught powerful glimpses of a different world outside, as well as discovering the possibility of choice.

Choice had little room in Jessie Kesson's early life. Born to a single mother, at a time when small-town society did not take too kindly to such aberrant conduct, she had her fill of institutional Big Houses — children's homes and orphanages. Such experience as she had of the more conventional 'Big', or 'Biggish' houses, in her early working years, were inevitably going to be from a below-stairs perspective.

Mitchison's young heroine (like Naomi herself?) developed an early social awareness from conversations overheard at the dinner-table of an unusually enlightened upper-class household. Jessie's youth was spent among those who were obliged to serve, for pennies. Her awarenesses came from direct experience. At the age of sixteeen, she exchanged the

bondage of the orphanage for that of employment as a servant, on a farm.

Those who have heard her speak, in her wonderfully unreconstructed North-East voice, will find it difficult to imagine that Jessie Kesson has lived for most of her long life in London, with the husband she met on that farm which provided her with her first full-time job. It's a long way from the loamy Black Isle, where they first settled, to literary friendships, in the great metropolis, with people like the poet Louis MacNeice. Jessie remembers each with equal affection.

She met Neil Gunn only once, when she was 'cottared at a farm near Cromarty', where her husband was cattleman. Gunn had written an approving postcard in response to a poem of hers which had appeared in the *Scots Magazine,* and invited her to visit him at Brae Farm, 'straight across the Firth.'

At that time she had begun sending verse and stories to the magazine, for which he contributed monthly episodes in a *Country Dweller's Year.* 'I felt a country "affinity" for his writing, which led me to reading his novels.' His work continues to provide stimulus. It refreshes her spirit, when it 'becomes city-jaded. Like taking a great quaff of cold water from his own *Drinking Well.'*

Jessie Kesson's fictional tribute to Gunn, *Cold in Coventry* is set in Sussex but could as easily be located in Skene, her own principal experience of orphanages, in rural Aberdeenshire. The institution and its routine are evoked with a subtle delicacy, yet the taste

of raw experience remains, unmistakable.

We are drawn into a world of petty rules, where communication is invariably from adult to child, in capital-lettered pronouncements. At times, as the title implies, even such social niceties are denied. When her young heroine is young enough to be sent out to her 'First Situation', service as scullery-maid in the local manor, we enter into an entirely different perspective of the world of the Big House, one of dirt, grease and overwhelming 'big oilskin aprons.'

Not having 'the *Makings* of a scullerymaid', the girl returns to the bleak institution, 'In Disgrace', the 'imprint of failure on her face'. But the human spirit is not so easily suppressed. Defiance is possible, the secret parody of that which Authority reveres. There is the eternal possibility of laughter.

Neil Gunn may have been the first Highland writer to connect with Oriental ways of looking at things, around a time when Japanese scholars were discovering many startling affinities between their own culture and that of the early Celts. The Zen evocation of the 'sound of one hand clapping' finds a harmonic in Fionn MacCumhail's assertion that the 'music of what happens is sweetest in the world.' Gunn, of course, found much to tease his imagination in the little book, *Zen in the Art of Archery*, by a German professor, Eugen Herigel.

Other Highland writers have since made similar journeys of the mind. Norman Malcolm Macdonald, Canadian-born Lewisman, refers to the Chinese *Tao*,

rather than Japanese Zen. The message he receives, the perceptions it allows him, are essentially the same.

Poet, novelist, historian and dramatist, in both his languages, MacDonald first came to public notice with his novel in English, *Calum Tod*. Later, the pioneering professional Gaelic theatre company *Fir Chlis* opened its brief existence with a production of his extra-ordinarily intense and poetic play *Anna Chaimbeul*.

This was a transmutation into drama of a traditional Gaelic song, *Ailean Duinn* (Brown-haired Allan). The theme of love ending in tragedy was a common one, uncommonly treated, by songmaker and playwright alike. MacDonald freely borrowed symbols and tech-niques from Japanese *Noh* theatre, to render his version of the story as spare and essential as the song, without losing any of its force.

The Shutter Falls has appeared in several manifesta-tions, as a play for stage, radio and television. Now, the author has distilled its contents down to a poem. This is a poem of episodes, quotations, evocations, which recreates, with fragile delicacy, the cama-raderie, toil and pride so characteristic of the lives of coastal herring girls in the first half of this century. These dignified island girls would have been familiar figures to the East Coast fishermen who went out in search of the 'Silver Darlings.'

Robin Jenkins is of the same generation as Jessie Kesson, if of a different geographic background. Migrations form a subtext to much Highland lit-erature. Jenkins is unusual in that he migrated *in*,

from Cambuslang, in Lanarkshire, to Cowal, where he taught in the local Grammar school, and where he remains in retirement.

While he has often used the urban Scottish environment of his early childhood, or his experience of Afghanistan, Malaysia and Spain, in his novels Jenkins has also frequently used Cowal, and other Highland locations. *The Cone Gatherers* and *The Changeling* are set in his adopted district, while *Fergus Lamont* brings its eponymous anti-hero to a kind of partial reconciliation in a remote and isolated community somewhere in the Uists.

Like Neil Gunn, Jenkins is much concerned with the nature of innocence, if from a broadly less optimistic perspective. *The Cone Gatherers* has certain affinities with *The Green Isle of the Great Deep*. Unlike young Art, his innocent, Calum, is physically deformed and mentally retarded, but he occupies a symbolic place in a piece of modern myth-making arising from the same war that so preoccupied Gunn. Duror's local fascism may ultimately destroy itself, but it is at the expense of Calum's life.

There is a Big House, again, in *The Cone Gatherers*, although we generally see it from the outside. Likewise 'Goatfell House' in *The Greengrocer and the Hero*, Robin Jenkins' story for this anthology. But now, it is only 'one of the mansions in Ailsa Park,' the very select residential area overlooking the town.

Lunderston, the municipality at the centre of this mordantly humorous tale, may share certain features with Dunoon, including an American military

presence in the background, but it could be any similar small town in the Highlands. Its shades of bourgeois pride, Presbyterian hypocrisy, and civic awareness are moderate enough not to shame any respectable burgh of its kind.

There are some marvellously comic moments, as the central character, Councillor Jack Rankin, narrow of perspective and smelling of apples, seeks a kind of justice for his daughter, carelessly impregnated in youth by the son of Goatfell House's incomer owners. This anarchic character disappears for a decade, then, after some shambolic mercenary activity in the Indian Ocean, revisits his home, a somewhat tainted hero. After a final, enigmatic, confrontation with the visitor, there is, for our stolid local hero, a curiously transcendental personal enlightment.

The poet and playwright Donald Campbell shares with our dedicatee the fact of birth in the county of Caithness, although he has spent most of his life in Edinburgh. While the capital city may have formed his day-to-day perceptions though, Campbell has kept one foot and at least half a soul in the North. Like most country-connected folk, he had a childhood of summers with the relations. As a young man with literary aspirations, he met Gunn in Edinburgh, and has a grandmother of that name in his kenning.

In poetry and in drama, Donald Campbell has often incorporated his knowledge of that Northerly low-land county of his forefathers into a muscular body of work that places him among the leading Scottish

writers of his generation. In each medium he has shown himself to be a vigorous exponent of the Nation's two principle non-Celtic languages, Scots and English. Not himself a Gaelic speaker, despite his name, he has learnt enough to be able to translate, into English and Scots, several works by the great Sutherland satirical poet, Rob Donn Mackay.

His first two plays, *The Jesuit* and *Somerville the Soldier*, were focussed on Central Lowland historical figures. With his third drama, he took as great a risk as any playwright of Celtic (however partial) or coastal provenance could take. His theme was the effect of a fishing tragedy on the women of a small isolated community. No pastiche, his *Widows of Clyde* rode the sea of critical apprehension to a harbour of deserved acclaim.

The Cutting-Off Piece, his submission to this collection, is another play with a strong Caithness accent. It also features one of our Highland area archetypes, an emigrant. Johnny Mackay, son of Dalmachair, finding himself quickly destitute on the rainsoaked streets of turn of the century Glasgow, encounters the Caithness witch, Jenny Horne. She empowers him with the ability to inhabit his own dreams.

Those visions are, inevitably, of home, friends, lovers, familiar things. But how familiar? The opportunity to step out of real time into another reality of dream time, does not ensure control of what is seen. When the familiar is viewed from outside, it may be lent a different, not always comforting perspective. Home is not necessarily a place to go back to. It

INTRODUCTION

remains, however, a place that can be carried in the mind, a loam for the imagination.

The youngest writer in this book is also the most Northerly in origin. Born in Shetland, he's been an emigrant four times. Three times back, and based in Edinburgh, he now reckons it's time to let his homeland be that place in the mind. Elsewhere is the environment he wants to inhabit meantime, to 'encounter fresh worlds and experiences.'

Being home and leaving home, are the themes that have much preoccupied him as a writer, as they have many an island writer, as indeed they concerned mainlander Gunn, one of three Scottish novelists he cites as influences. The Shetlandic language, 'an uneasy combination of English, Lowland Scots and Norrœna (Norn)', is also an important element in his writing.

He admits to creating a 'synthetic Shetlandic, using some Norn words and phrases bound together with Scots'. But 'their creation has not been entirely contrived'. Many of the less common words 'are familiar to me from my childhood in the isolated townships of Sannis — thanks to my great-grandmother... My close relationship with her has provided a connection with an older Shetland I might otherwise not have known.'

In *The Last Black Hoose* we are brought into contact with that older Shetland. It can be heard immediately, in the dialogue between 'Fædar' and the returning 'Boy'. It's there also, and its vulnerability, in the reported death on the previous evening, of 'Aald

Robbie o Snusquoy', occupant of the 'last black hoose in the toonship', with the two sisters, 'one of them that couldn't talk and the other that wouldn't.'

The boy has returned, in some trepidation, to announce that he does not intend to go back to university, thus breaking the wishes of his late mother, whose effects remain undisturbed by the widower. As father (a wool trader) and son sort and grade fleeces from surrounding farms, blackface and cheviot mostly, one fleece is discovered of pure Shetland wool. It becomes symbolic of what they themselves represent, an affirmation. There's a Big House in this story, but it's 'the derelict Haa, where the Lairds of old had lived.' There are other markets for optimism as well.

The author of the second contribution in verse is also a native Gaelic speaker. Spending the first decade of life in a small village in North Skye, in the years before mains electricity — and therefore before television or even extensive use of radio — a child might be expected to have heard something of the Gaelic tradition, in song or story. This child didn't, or certainly doesn't recall hearing such things, although I now know they were around. I do recall hearing psalms and bible-stories, and Free Church elders campaigning against the building of a community hall in the village. There would be dancing, and songs would be sung. And that wasn't proper.

Life wasn't quite so bleak. It seldom is, consistently. The community hall was built, and it had mains

electricity. I do not think I am wrong, however, in believing that the church I grew up in sought to annihilate any trace of their own culture and traditions from the minds of its adherents. It was many years before I began to put together fragments of the myth and lore which underlay my language, and my being. It took even longer to place that rich treasury of Gaelic tradition in a wider context, to realise that it shared motifs and patterns with many of the world's folklores.

I don't think I read anything of Gunn while he was alive. By the time reprints gave me access to his novels, I had made contact with both the recent history of my own people — the Clearances, in particular, through John Prebble's popular account initially — and with many other literatures available in accessible translations. These incuded Japanese poetry and Zen texts.

Discovering later that Gunn had also found affinities in the culture of that remote land gave a kind of validation to my own interest. He saw no incongruity in attempting to assimilate Zen concepts into a philosophical construction wrought from his own experience. That experience, it has to be remembered, was grounded in a deep knowledge of Gaelic folklore and history.

The sequence of short poems I present here, as homage to Neil Gunn, is written with a consciousness of the Japanese way of seeing things. They are not written in a specifically Japanese style. What is at least Japanese about them is a concern for nature, and an

attempt at simplicity. It's difficult for a Gael to avoid a preoccupation with history, when so much of our own has been effectively proscribed. Three histories are touched on here, those of the Gael, the Native American and the Ainu. The latter are a distinct people, of whom perhaps, 15,000 remain, defiantly hanging on to the remaining fragments of their culture, in the North Japanese island of Hokkaido.

Bess Ross is the *newest* writer in the present company. More than most, she is happy to acknowledge her debt to Neil Gunn. Always a reader, she grew upon a diet of Westerns and American thrillers. Then she became curious about her own tradition. Gunn was, with Jessie Kesson, Grassic Gibbon, and Mackay Brown, one of a range of authors who brought her in touch with Scottish literature for the first time.

What particularly excited her about these writers was that they were writing specifically from their own environments. Though ranging from Orkney to the Mearns, those environments were immediately and personally recognisable to herself. Her birthplace, Hilton of Cadboll, one of the seaboard villages of Easter Ross, has traditionally looked to the sea for its livelihood, but has also frequently depended on the large farms behind it for seasonal employment.

Her debt to Neil Gunn though, is more specific yet. She was a forty-two year old grandmother, sitting alongside a fifth year class at Tain Royal Academy, preparing for her Higher English exam, when she heard that Ross and Cromarty District Council had established a Neil Gunn Memorial literary competi-

tion. At the time, she was working on her first piece of fiction, a short story called *My Footprints in the Sand*.

In 1988, that story made her the first winner of the Neil Gunn Memorial Prize. Two years later, her first collection of short stories, *A Bit of Crack and Car Culture* appeared. Taking her mentors as markers, she has trawled, from memory and imagination, a fat and vibrant harvest of stories. Bess Ross has since written a novel, *Those Other Times*.

Her piece for this anthology, *The Big Boat*, is a deceptively simple account of three generations of fisherfolk, perceived essentially through the vision of Jake, who looks back to his own father, and encourages his sons, as they repair a newly purchased boat. Though the story ends at Jake's funeral, it is a celebration of continuity.

A funeral dominates our final contributor as well. Its author, Iain Crichton Smith is, in many ways the most various writer among us. Best known as a poet and novelist, in both Gaelic and English, he has also written plays, for stage and radio, in both languages.

Smith is a most prolific writer. It is not uncommon, glancing through his bibliography, to see four works appearing in a year, two in Gaelic, perhaps, and two in English. One may be a novel, one a play and two collections of poems or short stories. What is extraordinary about this river of work is that it is virtually never less than competent, always fluent, and sometimes quite magical in its grip on the reader's imagination. A poem like *Tha thu air aigeann m'inntinn/* 'You

are at the bottom of my mind' will surely resonate through all of time, as will his many poems in English which feature old women.

Assessing his poetry, in a long essay, Robin Fulton isolates the range of themes which preoccupy Smith into four general areas:

1 social criticism, ranging from small-town *mores* to world events;

2 the ambivalent qualities of power, will and intelligence;

3 the language and identity of his own Gaelic background;

4 loneliness, death, the hard honest facing of these, and the inadequacy of our defences.'

While Smith and Gunn differ in many aspects of their concerns, we may assume that the older writer would certainly have identified closely with the second and third areas specified. He would also have seen the relevance to his own prose of Smith's assertion concerning the 'greatest poetry', that it is 'created at the moment when you are at the frontiers. That is to say, when you are absorbing and transforming new material, that is, material which hasn't been transformed before....'

Paradoxically, although Gunn's *Butcher's Broom* and Smith's *Consider the Lilies* draw on the same basic material, incidents in that tragic tide of events we call the Highland Clearances, their treatment of it is quite individual. Each succeeds in transforming it with equal force and artistry.

The Red Coffin is Iain Crichton Smith's gift for Gunn,

which brings this anthology to a vivid, mysterious and joyous conclusion. It begins in the exasperated real world of a mother dealing with the visions of her apparently fanciful son. Together, they take us out of the story, out through a transcendentally surreal space that is altogether sunshine and joy.

There is a dialogue in this story, ordinary, everyday, episodic dialogue. There is descriptive prose, precise and detailed in its observation, but prose. It is not a poem. It is a story. Yet at the end, while everything is explained, nothing is explained. It is all planted in our imagination, like a poem. This is material transformed, new material 'which hasn't been transformed before.'

Had the purpose of this book been to represent the full range and quality of writing from the Highlands and Islands, many more authors would have had to be included. The world of Gaelic alone has seen a remarkable literary flowering in the second half of this century: the youngest writer in a recent anthology is still in her early twenties.

In that they are still major literary figures, by any reckoning, the absence *is* regretted of two particular writers, whose achievements are recognised far beyond this region which claims them for its own. Raasay-born Sorley MacLean, whose poems are steely filaments of Gaelic history, and Norman MacCaig, born in Edinburgh to a Harris Gaelic mother, and forever laureate of Assynt, both regretted having nothing new to offer. MacCaig had written no new poems since the death of his wife. MacLean's work

on further sections of his long poem-in-progress, *The Cave of Gold*, was still unfinished.

That MacLean and MacCaig both shared many concerns and perceptions with Gunn is manifest in their work. Poems like MacCaig's *Toad* and *Praise of a Collie*, or MacLean's *Coin is Madaidhean-Allaidh/* 'Dogs and Wolves' and *Hallaig* testify to a deep intimacy with the landscape they have inhabited, its flora and fauna, its people and its memories. There is a trans-forming quality to so much of the work of both poets, that is sometimes dark, intense, and always brilliant. They may not be here, but their collected works are in print, and are commended.

Ten contributors may, after all, be an apt number for this book, one for each decade since the birth of Neil Gunn. The oldest, Naomi Mitchison, was born in the same decade as her old friend. The newest, though not youngest, Bess Ross, was first published in his centenary decade. Through all their words, a broad and many-textured canvas of twentieth cen-tury life in the Highlands has been painted. Through all their works, the creative vitality of the area is affirmed, and tribute is gladly paid to the memory, gift, and influence of that great Scottish novelist of Highland birth, Neil Miller Gunn.

Aonghas MacNeacail — April 1991

INTRODUCTION

THE VOYAGE OF THE FLOOD-TIDE

George Mackay Brown

I T HAPPENED ONE SPRING THAT a merchant ship left Orkney for the town of Grimsby in England. This ship, called '*Flood-Tide*', had a cargo of best Norwegian timber and walrus-bone. It had been agreed with an English merchant the previous winter that '*Flood-Tide*' would carry back to Orkney a cargo of English wool and casks of cider.

There is nothing in any way remarkable to tell about the crew of '*Flood-Tide*'. The skipper was a sullen man, and the seven sailors under him were passable seamen. When they were ashore and got drunk, even then there was little in the way of fun or fighting or fantasy in them.

"A dull ship, that '*Flood-Tide*,'" said the Kirkwall merchants. "But very reliable, and Sven the skipper the most honest of men."

Like all islanders, the crew loved stories even better than ale or girls. But not one had skill in the telling of tales.

"That will be a dull voyage, all the way to Grimsby

and back," said a Scapa beachcomber.

'Flood-Tide' left Kirkwall with a fair wind, and Sven the skipper negotiated well the intricate streams and whirls of the Pentland Firth, but when the ship rounded John o' Groats the wind backed south and east and strengthened.

"We'll have to shelter in some bay," said Sven. "A waste of time."

It happened that in Orkney, at the last minute before sailing, an oarsmen called Valt had fallen in slippery seaweed and broken his leg.

So they asked a boy standing on the jetty if he would sail with them. Sven had noted that this youth was good with ropes and sails, and he seemed to be a friend of the sea.

The boy said he would have to get permission from his mother.

"I wouldn't have anything to do with that boy," said a sailor called Hrut. "His mother is Branda and everybody knows she is a witch."

"He doesn't seem to me to have an unlucky look about him," said the skipper.

The boy came down from the village and said his mother gave permission for him to sail on 'Flood-Tide'. "I think Branda will be glad to see the back of me for a while", he said.

Then he laughed so cheerfully that some faces of that dull crew smiled in reply.

But Sven frowned more severely than before.

"Remember," said he, "you will have to work hard on your passage, and there will be little laughter once we're out in the North Sea gales."

The boy, whose name was Simon, said he would expect a wage like every sailor.

Then Sven told him not to be impudent and to jump on board and carry out orders promptly.

When the south-east gale struck them, south of John o' Groats, two or three of the seamen said it was bad luck to have Branda's son on board, for he must be tainted with witchcraft.

"It's true I have the second sight," said the boy, Simon, "but I only see things that are good and true, and I'm glad of that."

"You work well enough," said Sven the skipper. "An ill wind can blow at any time."

A sailor called Tor said, between howls of wind, that there was a fishing village called Dunbeath, and they could ride out the storm in that small bay.

"Besides," said Tor, "I know for a fact there is a great story-teller in that village called Njal Gunnison, and so we might be well entertained for an evening or two."

Sven grumbled that the Dunbeath fishermen would want a few Norwegian staves and stobs from their cargo for sheltering them, and the story-teller would want a silver coin for sure.

They saw Dunbeath through a smother of foam,

but Sven brought the ship in safely to the voe and cast anchor.

The villagers, once they knew for sure that the 'Flood-Tide' was not a viking ship, came down to the shore and invited the crew to their fires and tables.

The crew of the Orkney ship were well entertained in the house of the chief man in Dunbeath, a farmer called Donal.

The wind still howled outside, shaking the door.

After the meal of bread and fish and ale, served by Donal's three daughters, the village folk came shyly into the house, and stood here and there, wanting to hear news from Orkney. But Sven told them little.

But the youngest sailor, Simon, after a mug of ale, spoke easily and pleasantly to the Dunbeath folk, so that they laughed at his gossip.

Then the sailor Hrut said to Simon, "You've drunk too much ale. We would like to hear another voice for a change."

Then there was silence in the house, except that old Donal kept urging hospitality on the strangers.

Tor refused an oatcake and cheese. He went on. "We hear there's a famous story-teller here in Dunbeath, Njal Gunnison. It would be a joy to hear a story from that enchanting mouth."

"You have come a day too late," said the host. "The

story-teller has gone south to Inverness. The man in the little castle there has had six barrels of usquebaugh delivered to him by a man in the west who makes that wild fiery stuff, a great vat of it, each winter. The castellan in Inverness, though he thinks himself a fine judge of good food and drink, is really a stupid man with only a crude taste in his mouth, and he frequently buys gut-rot usque, and stinking salmon, so he doesn't get so many guests in his hall as formerly. It is well known that Njal from Dunbeath here, is the finest judge of usque in the north, and so he has been sent for to advise the thick-mouthed castellan about the six barrels from the west."

"When will the famous story-teller and judge of drink be back?" said Tor.

"That is hard to say" said Donal. "He takes his time. He is kept at every clachan and smithy between Inverness and here so that the folk can listen with joy to his beautiful words. Over and over again he has to recite the tales of the salmon, the galaxies of herring, and the well of wisdom at the world's end. Njal may be home in another month, but by then the storm will have abated and you will be doing business in the busy booths along the waterfront at Grimsby."

A gloom fell on all the company once they understood that they might never have a chance of hearing the famous stories of Njal Gunnison, told by the man himself.

Just then a small boy entered from the wind and rain, but when he saw the strangers he turned and

would have run out again if one of Donal's daughters hadn't grabbed him and set him down on a stool beside the fire. The child would only look into the flames.

By now they could tell by the sound of the wind in the roof-vent, that the storm was lessening. The door ceased to rattle. "I think," said the old man Donal, "the wind is shifting into the north. You will be able to sail on south in the morning."

"Speak to the Orkneymen," said one of the daughters of the house to the child who was still looking into the the flames and shadows.

But the child said nothing.

"I would like another mug of ale," said Simon, the young Orkney sailor.

Donal's youngest daughter poured him ale from her tall jug. Simon Brandason sat looking hard at the flame-lapped boy.

"What is the name of that boy?" he said.

"His name is Sweyn," said the girl Maurya. "His mother is called Asleif. She is a fine woman, Asleif."

She went on, "The boy is called after his mother, Sweyn Asleifson, because his father, Olaf Rolfson, all but disowns him. Olaf says he is ashamed to have fathered such a strange useless son. The child Sweyn seems to be interested in nothing worthwhile. He won't go near the fishing boats or the barns where the men are threshing. He says hardly a word to anyone. Olaf his father thinks he will become a man of no account, a beggar or a beachcomber."

The boy Sweyn sat on the stool and looked into the fire and it seemed he had no interest in all the talk about him.

Simon took another mouthful of ale, till his curled golden beard was all frothed, and he said, "This Sweyn is a most extraordinary child. He will do great things when he comes to manhoood."

Still the child Sweyn looked into the fire, as if he were reading images and runes there.

The men and women of Dunbeath laughed at the idea that Sweyn would ever do anything more remarkable than sit chewing cold ashes.

"He will sit at the right hand of the Earl at Orphir in Orkney at midwinter," said Simon. "I can see that. That very night he will turn his axe against the Earl's bodyguard and cut him down. Then I see him riding away from the Hall in Orphir, under the stars, to the shore of Firth, and sailing on from there to Egilsay. In Egilsay — the island of Magnus's martyrdom — he will be received well and courteously by the Bishop of Orkney."

The people of Dunbeath laughed louder than ever.

The skipper of 'Flood-Tide' looked severely at the youngest man in his crew.

The child Sweyn whom no-one took seriously seemed untouched by those fore-shadowings, looking with wonderment at the sparks flying from the new-laid peats.

"He is an innocent, he understands nothing," said Bridget the second daughter of the house.

Simon took another draught of ale and said, "This Sweyn here, he will soon after that become the most powerful man in Orkney — he will move earl against earl as if they were chessmen on a board."

The Caithness people mocked no longer, for now it seemed to them that Simon Brandason might be uttering words of truth that were hidden from other men.

Even Simon's voice was changed now, as if he was chanting mildly and monotously through a mask, and was possibly not aware of what he himself was saying.

Only Sven the skipper kept muttering, "He doesn't know how to hold his drink. Simon Brandason will never sail on a ship of mine again."

The mild voice of the witch's son went on, "Sweyn will have a large estate in Orkney, on an island there with a hall and a farm under a green hill. The estate will be so prosperous and well-managed that it will maintain eighty men, shepherds and fishermen, smiths and farmworkers, carpenters and builders besides, of course, a host of women-folk and children. The fertile island will be well stocked with cattle, sheep, swine, pigeons, and the tides round it will be crowded with fish — haddock and mackerel and lobsters. Sweyn will sit there at the high table in winter, a benign and just laird, and after the supper cauldrons and platters have been cleared away, a

skald will strike the harp and recite the exploits of the hero."

The child Sweyn had fallen asleep with his blond head in the lap of Solveig the youngest daughter.

"I have never heard such nonsense," said Sven the skipper severely. "The earl in Birsay would never allow an Orkneyman to have such power. It would be a danger to himself and to the whole earldom. The king in the east, in Norway, would have something to say about it too. Your Caithness ale has shaken much folly from this man's mouth."

"Yet I think we should go on listening to what Simon says," said Donal. "I have known men who called themselves seers, and they uttered enough folly, but this young sailor has the star of prophecy on his forehead, it seems to me."

Now Donal's three daughters had come to sit around the sleeping child, and one stroked his hand gently and one let her fingers drift through the gold clusters of his head and one sat at his feet and looked at the face that had drifted into innocent sleep.

"Yes," said Simon, his mild chant gathering strength, "the skald will sing of a hero, for in the isle of Sweyn Asliefson it is not tranquillity and increase always, year after year, as if the golden age had come. Men perform the rituals of peace — ploughing and sowing and harrowing. Are they then to lounge about the glebe all summer waiting for harvest, beyond rainbows and the sun's slow burnish? No, they launch the longship, they drag her with ropes out of the shed where she has slept all winter among mice and spiders, and she meets the sea with a glad silver splash. The women bring provisions and stock the hold well with smoked hams and trout and cheese, and some of the younger women are weeping and the mouths of some of the older women are full of mockery. And then the shepherds, blacksmiths, fishermen, stockmen, ploughmen, carpenters, once they are on shipboard, are all careless sailors, with the sea dazzle in their eyes. What are they waiting for? What keeps them from the rowing-benches? They wait for the chief to come out of the Hall, the hero, Sweyn Asliefson, last and greatest of the vikings."

The child Sweyn slept beside the hearth, guarded well by Maurya and Bridget and Solveig.

At mention of the word "viking" the Dunbeath men looked uneasily at each other; every village along that coast had suffered for generations from those sea-wolves; but the savagery and blood-letting and depredation had stopped since the good Earl Hakon had established his reign of peace over Orkney and all the territories of the north. Surely there would never be nests of such pirates again! Surely they had all been smoked out and their sinister secret bournes probed to the root, utterly and forever.

The Dunbeath men blanched, some of them, to think of what their fathers had suffered at the hands of the vikings.

Then old Donal looked across at the sleeping child who, it seemed, was to become the greatest viking of all, and he could not but smile. Surely the young Orkney seaman Simon Brandason was only telling a story after all — and there was no harm in that — a weaving on the loom of the imagination could pass an evening pleasantly enough.

"We have heard enough nonsense for one night," said Sven the skipper. "We should be getting down to the ship now. The weather has settled. Thank you for your hospitality."

But the villagers and the sailors of 'Flood-Tide' were eager for the story to be rounded out to a close. If they could not be entertained by the great Njal Gunnison, this Simon Brandason was doing well enough.

The story-teller had a recently replenished ale-mug at his elbow but he pushed it away from him, and his face had a pure grave sweet look on it that they had not seen before.

"At the tide's turning, Sweyn Asliefson goes to the ship, and the sail is set, and the ship drifts through Eynhallow Sound into the open ocean. All summer Gairsay is an island of women alone, except for a few grumbling old men and children going with bird-cries

between the hill and the shore. The corn ripens about the island of women, and the corn whispers change from green to gold, and the sheep are shorn and the abundant milk of the cows changed to butter and into great cheeses heavy as quernstones. And the women quarrel with each other more and more often as the weeks pass, but always there is a woman down at the shore shading her eyes north and west. At last a strange sail is sighted, a sail striped azure and black and crimson. The hull veers in toward the island, now the women — seventy women, crones and russet-faces and small girls — can see the faces of husbands and sons and fathers, and there at the helm Sweyn Asleifson himself, the sea magic in his eyes. Every August there are a few faces missing from the rowing-bench, and a few women weep in secret. But most years there is great rejoicing as the silver plate and bales of wool and casks of wine and rolls of Spanish leather are spread out on the shore. It has been, again, a great viking cruise into the west. Then after a few days for rest and celebration, the sickles are taken out of the barn and the cobwebs blown from them and the vikings change themselves into harvesters. The blades flash in the sun of late summer. Sweyn the laird, the viking chief, friend of earl and bishop and king, his scythe seems to make purer brighter keener circles than all the others. They will not lack for bread and ale in Sweyn's island next winter.

"So it goes on year after year in that happy island: the ploughing and fishing, the viking cruise, the

harvesting, the winter of chess-playing and feasting and poetry.

"But at last there are white hairs in Sweyn's golden beard, and his eye dims so that he can no longer see his hawk over the hill, and in the cold weather he gets pains in his hip-bone and shoulder.

"His friends and councillors — even the earl himself — pleads with Sweyn to stay at home and make no more viking cruises. He has accumulated great fame and wealth. He ought to be content. Let him take his ease now.

" 'It will be a long enough sleep in the grave', said the old man Sweyn. 'It is true, I think death is not far off. Yet I would like to make one more cruise west and south. The blood in my veins still makes an eager response to the surge and flow of the ocean, especially when the spring tides go at full bore on either side of Eynhallow, the holy island. After the last voyage, I will be at peace, I promise you.'

"Sweyn Asleifson's words please them all.

"Soon it is time for ploughing in Gairsay. It is noticed that when the ox gave a sudden lurch in the furrow, the stilt of the plough falls from Sweyn's powerful hand. That has never happened before.

"When the last seed-bag was empty, Sweyn gave orders for the ship 'Ragna', newly caulked and planked and provisioned, to be sent down the rollers into the firth.

"He went on board, hirpling a little on account of the pain in his leg.

"With a great shout the sail was raised, and the 'Ragna' drifted with wind and tide out through Eynhallow Sound.

"The oldest women in Gairsay said, 'Sweyn Asleifson our good lord and master is not too long for this world. It will be a good thing to have his dust in a howe, here in Gairsay, but I think Sweyn will meet his death in a strange land far away'...

"The corn grew tall and green that summer, and the first glints of bronze were in the stalks when the girl who was keeping watch that day on the hillside ran down to the Hall and said that a ship with a black sail was rounding Scabra Head in Rousay.

"The old men, squinnying out to sea, recognized the cut of the 'Ragna' the viking ship.

"The crew were slow to come ashore. About half the crew were missing, and the rest looked gray and gaunt, like men who had had to linger for a winter among ice.

"The youngest crew-man came ashore, weeping. He told Sweyn's people that their lord had been struck down in the city of Dublin in Ireland. He had fallen into a cunningly-laid pit, he had drowned under a sea of swords and axes...

"There was silence in the island of Gairsay, for seven days. Even the women of the north think it wrong to raise outcries against the decrees of Fate. Let Fate make what it can of their silence.

"This is my story of the life and death of Sweyn Asliefson."

Simon fell silent.

"Well," said old Donal at last, "that was a good enough story to come from the mouth of an Orkneyman. Of course it lacked the Celtic weave of mystery".

The Dunbeath folk and the crew of 'Flood-Tide' clapped their hands.

The women went round again with the ale jars.

Then this happened, that a shudder went through Simon the story-teller, and he rubbed his eyes. "I must have gone to sleep," he said. "It is the good ale you keep here in Dunbeath. I had a very strange dream too, but what it was about I don't remember."

Maurya Donalsdottor poured ale into Simon's mug until the foam stood high above the rim. "Well told, story-teller," she said.

At that very moment the child Sweyn awoke. He raised his head from Solveig's lap and looked with startled eyes round the people in the house, especially at the strangers, the Orkneymen.

But then the eye of the child met the eye of the seer, and Sweyn Asleifson smiled.

"God be with you always, boy," said Simon Brandason.

Then the crew of the 'Flood-Tide' went down to the ship. They left three planks of well-seasoned timber on the shore to pay for the hospitality they had had in Dunbeath.

In the morning with a fair wind, they sailed on south.

Sven the skipper had some hard bargaining with the merchants on the Grimsby waterfront and came out of it better than expected.

The crew of the *'Flood-Tide'* kept to the ship for the most part. They seemed to have no interest in Grimsby or its streets and people.

Simon Brandason went missing for a night and a day. At last he came unsteadily down the long wharf and he looked hollow-eyed and dishevelled.

"You will never sail on a ship of mine again," said Sven. "I won't have drunkards on the rowing-bench."

They stowed the bales of wool and casks of apple-ale on board 'Flood-Tide' and secured them well, and waited for a fair wind to sail north.

"You will not visit any more taverns in Grimsby," Sven said to Simon. "I confine you to the ship.".

On the third morning they set sail. It was noticed that Simon Brandason was merrier than usual, and it seemed to some of the crew that he had managed to broach a cider cask during the night.

But Simon was well-liked by the sailors and nothing was said to the skipper.

Nothing is told of their voyage north until they rounded Kinnaird Head, and they ran into foul

weather and had their work cut out keeping the drenches of salt spray out of the wool bales.

"It may be," said Sven gloomily, "that we will have to shelter in some cove for a day or two. If we had got the cargo to Orkney early, the agreement was I would have been paid a higher fee."

Tor said, "Why don't we shelter in Dunbeath? We had a good welcome there on our way south."

Sven thought that was a good plan. "Only," said he, "the drunken sailor will stay and look after the ship. We don't want any more of his wild imaginings. Also, for his information, I have put an extra seal on the bung of every cider cask."

Simon looked downcast at those words. "I'd been hoping to have some talk with the three daughters of the house," he said. "But I'll do as you say, Sven."

They navigated the ship into the harbour at Dunbeath. The villagers recognized 'Flood-Tide' and they came down to welcome the crew.

"Indeed," said old Donal, "you must all come up to my house and warm yourselves at my fire. I think this strong north-easterly will soon blow itself out and you'll be able to sail to Orkney in the morning."

All the crew trooped up to Donal's house and they were hardly seated when the three daughters went round the seafarers with platters of cheese and new warm bread and the tall ale-jars.

"What has become of the handsome young sailor who sailed south in your ship?" said Maurya. "Where is the man who put such golden prophecies on the

boy Sweyn Asliefson?"

"I have confined him to the ship," said Sven sourly. "He did not behave here in Dunbeath all that well. In Grimsby he disgraced himself with drink entirely. It is better he sleeps under a thwart tonight."

In small groups, and shyly, all the Dunbeath people trooped into Donal's house to hear news of the great world beyond Caithness.

The sailors told them this and that, but none of them had any gift for the telling of news, so the Dunbeath folk had little pleasure from the mumbled scraps that fell from their mouths.

Donal's daughters lit the lamps and poured stronger ale into the jugs, in the hope that the tongues of the Orkneymen would be loosened.

But this good drink seemed only to make them gloomier.

"If we don't get to Kirkwall before the weekend," said Sven, "I might even have to forfeit part of my fee. This northerly, by the howl of it in the roof-vent, might last for a month."

But Donal assured him that the wind had more west than north in it now. "In the morning," he said, "it will be a brave south-westerly."

"And if you don't get your freight-silver," said the sailor called Hrut, "I suppose that means less wages for all of us. You're mean enough with our wages as things are, Sven."

It looked as though it might come soon to fighting among the seamen, for some of them had stood up

and were glaring at Sven and Sven was holding his alehorn as if he would strike anyone who came within range of him.

"They can't hold their drink," said a shepherd from Latheron. "They would have had a merrier evening with a bucketful of water from the burn."

At this point the door opened and a man came in that the Orkneymen had not seen before.

The man was greeted with glad cries from the villagers.

Donal's daughters made haste to bring in a fine oak chair and set it at the fire for the new visitor.

The Orkneymen looked rather ashamed of themselves and left off quarreling.

Maurya brought to the visitor an ale-horn that had silver mountings at the rim and the handle, and when Bridget poured the best ale into the horn, Solveig came behind with a pot of honey and added two spoonfuls to their drink.

"This guest who has honoured us with his presence," said Donal to the Orkneymen, "is the famous story-teller Njal Gunnison."

Then Donal turned to Njal and said, "The strangers in my house are sailors out of Orkney, peaceable merchantmen. They have had hard dangerous voyages, both going to Grimsby in England and now on the voyage home. Nothing is so sweet to sea-beaten sailors as a story well told."

Njal greeted the Orkneymen well. He seemed to

THE VOYAGE OF THE FLOOD-TIDE

the crew of 'Flood-Tide' a grave courteous man.

They raised their ale-mugs to him. The sailor Tor was so excited that he spilled some of his ale.

A silence fell on the house of Donal.

Out of the silence came the voice of the story-teller Njal.

He recited the story of the boy and the salmon — then the story of the galaxies of herring in the west — and last of all the story of the well of wisdom.

The Orkneymen listened, enchanted.

Even Sven the skipper's eyes opened in wonderment.

They could not have told if an hour had passed, or a whole night.

But the lamps were still burning, and Maurya was filling ale-jugs from the barrel set in the dark cold corner.

The Orkneymen looked around, after the long marvellous silence, and they saw that the chair of the story-teller Njal Gunnison was empty.

Sven said to Donal, "We thank you for this evening. I think, even in the Earl's hall on a feast day, in Birsay, there is no such joy as we poor sailors have had in your most hospitable house."

"It seems to me," said Donal, "that Celtic story-tellers have a special gift of weaving mystery and magic into their tales. It is very late now. I think you should lie down and sleep round my hearth till morning. Then you will be in good shape to face the hazards

of the Pentland Firth."

The Orkneymen lay about the hearth till daylight. Then they went down to the shore, and the Dunbeath people followed, with farewells on their lips.

"Drunkard!" cried Sven to the watchman, Simon. "Disgrace to the sea and ships and peaceful commerce! Bring a keg of English cider to our hosts here in Dunbeath. Bring a small keg. They might not care all that much for the English gut-rot."

So Simon let himself down into the shallow water with a keg of cider on his shoulder and he waded ashore.

Then Simon went to where the three daughters of Donal were standing and he set the keg down at their feet.

Maurya and Bridget and Solveig seemed pleased to see Simon.

"Now tell me," said Simon, "where is the boy Sweyn Asliefson who was here in Dunbeath last time we called here? I don't see him."

Maurya said that young Sweyn had gone back to his father's house in Duncansby.

"His mother Asleif no longer spoils the boy so much," said Bridget. "Sweyn stays away from the women's quarters now. He spends more time with his brothers. Now he can actually ride a horse over the strath."

"Yes," said Solveig, "and the child has been out in the lobster boat off Stroma, a very stormy place, and they say he had more lobsters in his creel than all the seasoned fishermen."

"The latest news we have of Sweyn," said Maurya, "is that his father Olaf has given him a hawk. This hawk, a fierce creature by all accounts, will come to nobody's hand but Sweyn's."

Sven the skipper shouted from the prow of 'Flood-Tide', "When you have finished gossiping on the shore, we can up anchor and be off."

Off Dunnet Head, Tor told Simon Brandason of the wonderful evening they had spent up at Donal's house, listening to the great stories of Njal Gunnison.

Simon said he was sorry to have missed that, and the Caithness ale that was so good, and also the company of the three beautiful daughters of Donal.

THE CAMPAIGN AGAINST BLONC

Naomi Mitchison

T IS DIFFERENT GOING TO STAY with Aunt Gertie and Uncle James and of course Grandma but she does not come down for Breakfast. We have what Nurse calls family lunch with them, but we sit at a table for ourselves and we are not allowed some of the grown-up things, but we are by the big window so we can see the peacocks and lots of other birds and sometimes a deer. It is the country and if you can get away, but they do so hold our hands, you can go up the hill and into the bracken, right down where the rabbits live and there will be wild pansies and woodruff and golden-rod and all the little paths and holes for the mice. These are not like the house mice who nibble our bread and the grown-ups cheese, and make holes in the tops of the big pots of marmalade for grown-up breakfast and sometimes in the big porridge bag so that the oatmeal runs out on the floor and Mrs Cook talks about leaving unless the out-door mice are good mice.

THE CAMPAIGN AGAINST BLONC

And there is Blonc which means white in French. Aunt Gertie told us that. Going to stay with Aunt Gertie and the others means meeting Blonc and I am going to tell you about our war with Blonc, so you must know that he is a very big dog, thick looking and whitish all over after he has been under the tap and dried and combed, and he comes from Switzerland, the part where they talk French and there is lots of white snow and people fall into it and can't get out unless dogs like Blonc find them and pull them out and carry them home. The Blonc dogs have collars with bottles of brandy, which Uncle James likes almost as well as whisky, and it is very good for people if they get very cold like they do if they fall into the snow and can't get out.

All this is in Switzerland which is in my geography book and there is a Blonc mountain called after the white dogs. I suppose it has lots of dogs like him running up and down it. So I must tell you more about Blonc and about us and him because even before we began packing we were talking about him and about our war. That is, mostly, my big brother Edward, which is the same name as the King's and my little brother Johnnie. But we know when we get there we have the cousins and I know that whatever we plan, they plan differently at first, but then they see we are right. But just sometimes we think that they are right. But we know they agree with us about Blonc.

The worst thing Blonc does and he has done it a lot of times, is to knock us over and then pick us up

and carry us to where Uncle James is. He doesn't truly bite us, only he slobbers over my frock and Johnnie's knickerbockers and everyone laughs, all the grown-ups I mean, and say what a clever doggie he is. But he is not really clever, he only likes to think he is rescuing us from the snow and there is never snow in the summer holidays. But Uncle James laughs at us so much I really and truly hate him, and to be carried by a dog is very uncomfortable for me and Johnnie and for my cousin Millie and her brother Henry, and she often cries about it, but they tell her not to be Silly-Milly which is their unkind name.

Blonc does other things. He has been taught to lift a paw to shake, but he does not see when his paw is muddy, so he has sometimes put a muddy paw onto ladies' skirts and once he did it to a visitor who was a bishop and wears black silk stockings, but thicker than ladies' and his big paw scratched a huge hole in the bishop's stocking and Edward and me found it very difficult not to laugh. Johnnie did laugh but he is only five so it doesn't count.

The grown-ups were very upset, at least they pretended to be, but afterwards I heard Uncle James telling it as a funny story. The other thing that Blonc did was to wag a whole comb of garden honey off the tea table and Jane the parlour maid took ages mopping it up. Still it was nice, because that comb was broken and didn't look right, so they had to have another for drawing room tea and we had the broken one for nursery tea, that is, most days, so it was a

happy ending and we wished he would do it again,
but he never did.

I like it when Aunt Gertie tells Nurse we are to
come down for drawing room tea on Saturday and
Sunday. It is much nicer and she doesn't make us
have bread and butter first before shortbread or
cherry cake. I hope she will always do it. But sometimes she asks difficult questions like did we have
nice dreams, and that made me instead remember my
bad dreams, and some seem to be about Blonc.

I talk with Aunt Gertie about all sorts of things, as
though she was not a grown-up and would never
laugh at me, as if she was one of us. The last time we
came she told me about her travels and how she went
to India in a huge ship with a great engine in the
middle. She showed me things she had brought back
from India like the little table that the newspapers
live on and the finger bowls that look so nice all round
the table, and the silk scarf that she let me pull
through a ring. She met Indian ladies who wore
beautiful clothes and some spoke good English, but
sometimes they got burnt.

I know she went to Africa too, but when I asked
she didn't tell me much and she only brought back a
few beads. I said did she see the Boers and she said
yes, but then she began to talk quickly about something else. That is called changing the subject. But I
think it is difficult to do without being rude. Anyhow
I know the Boers are bad people. My Mama told me
they killed one of our cousins. But he was not a very
nice one, Mama said. I know that some far-off people

are good. The Japanese won a war against the Russians although they are smaller, and they are good and make lovely paper animals and flowers out of paper and beautiful kites. They are not in the Empire, as India is, so they don't belong. That's all I know about them.

We got here yesterday and I was a little sick in the train, but not very. Only Nurse was cross and didn't let me have any cake, though some had been sent in and when Aunt Gertie came to see that everything was all right, Nurse went stiff and made Aunt Gertie feel uncomfortable. I tried to signal to her but couldn't. I am not sick now and I want to go up the hill but Nurse wouldn't let me. She gave me a grey powder before she put me to bed. It was a nasty one and I had to get up early and run. And I almost finished the paper. But Nurse said there is nothing like a good turn-out and perhaps she'd give me another. So if I am sick again I will go out into the bushes and hide it and wash my face. I did so want to go up the hill by myself.

Perhaps tomorrow if Nurse is fussing over Baby I shall be allowed to go. I think Baby is often naughty on purpose but Nurse thinks not. I want to take Johnnie with me up the hill. He is old enough. Five

is old enough. Cousin Henry is almost six, but Cousin Millie is seven like me, only her birthday comes after mine. I do not mind that, but I want it to be me alone who takes Johnnie up the hill.

I have been to the greenhouse with Aunt Gertie. She showed me the begonias. The she-begonias have big green bags behind them to hold the seeds which are their babies. The he-begonias are prettier. Aunt Gertie gave me a twig off one. It was very good. This time, when she went away, she was in France looking at cathedrals. But cathedrals are only big churches, so it sounds very dull.

Now the cousins come to tea. Ursula wears nearly grown-up clothes and only talks to Agnes, who is my older sister. They talk to one another secretly. I hear Ursula say, Oh Edith won't understand. Edith is me. But I do understand everything they talk about. They got giggly about something that the Vicar had said and it was in the Bible, but somehow it sounded funny. I don't think they ought to have laughed about it and never told me just what it was.

Then the rest of the cousins came and we all started talking about Blonc. I mean not the babies, nor Johnnie and Henry who are not yet at a proper school like I am, with Latin tenses and geography. So we got inside the Big Bush where you can crawl between the low branches and it is a house. The boys had some toffee for all of us. There is a very old bench there with beetles and a wobbly table.

I said we were like Parliament to help people in

trouble and send out armies. But then Cousin Herbert and our Edward began to say they were special people called Ministers and then they started arguing and got silly. So we got back to Blonc and how he had already pushed Johnnie over and picked him up with his teeth so that there were slobber marks on Johnnie's new knickers. Nurse had already scolded Edward about this, but how could Edward alone have stopped Blonc? — who kept wagging his tail as if we ought to be pleased with him. He had carried Johnnie over nearly to Uncle James and then Uncle had laughed and told poor Johnnie not to blub about nothing. But it is not nothing to be bullied by Blonc.

So we all knew it was no good saying anything to Uncle James. We would have to stop Blonc ourselves. He is our enemy, so perhaps we should give him an enemy name so that the grown-ups wouldn't know who we were talking about. Then Herbert said DOG backwards was GOD, but I thought that was a dreadful thing to have said. Then we talked about other enemies, but none of us were quite sure who our real enemies are because the empire is all the red bits all round the world and the rest doesn't count and anyway we don't know their names. I think Russians used to be our enemies and there is a poem about the gallant six hundred, but that was quite long ago and then there was the Indian Mutiny and there is an old gentleman who sometimes comes to tea and Mama told me he was very brave and held a fort somewhere. But it was a long time ago. Once he showed me his medals and told me a lot of names

which I have forgotten. Aunt Gertie says that Indian ladies are as kind and as clever as English ladies only much more beautiful.

So in the end the boys decided what to call Blonc and it was False Sextus because he was always doing deeds of shame like knocking people over. But I thought it was silly because the grown-ups would know we were talking about their dog and they would laugh at us. That was what did happen and it didn't last for long. So sucks for the boys.

Aunt Gertie has been away for a few days but she will be back soon. I heard the grown-ups talking about her and Uncle James said she was putting her finger into a hot pie, which I couldn't understand as she doesn't get into the kitchen much. But I think she is doing something brave, because Grannie told Uncle James he was not to laugh at his niece who was doing something truly brave and worthy of the family. Uncle James tittered a little but he shut up.

With her away we are back to nursery tea and there is only raspberry jam. But Mrs Cook sometimes comes in and last time she brought a cake with sultanas and cherries and gave me a second slice in spite of Nurse. I do like the kitchen and the kitchen maids who come in from the farms and when they get married Uncle James always gives them a present though I think it is only money, which is a dull present. I like Solly Sticky at the home farm. But it is not his real name, which I know is Solomon like in the Bible and I know he goes to the other church; I think they are called Methodists. I like Solly Sticky's wife who gives me a spoonful of cream if I go to their house and she has a canary. He has a lot of sheep. I am sorry for them when all their wool is cut off. But I suppose it has to be if I am to have a new winter coat. At least that is what Nurse says.

Another person I like is Simon the butler who is rather old and who lets me help him clean the silver and he showed me how to mend things carefully with glue. He has been here for years and years when there were only candles. Now it is lamps but they have a kind of thing inside which breaks very easily, so I must not touch it, but it makes a nice bright light. We have electric lights at home but the electricity has not come as far as here and I am allowed to have a candle on the mantelpiece left alight when I am asleep, but sometimes it burns out before morning and I hate it when I wake and it is dark and dreams are waiting to catch me. Johnnie was sleeping with me but this year he has been moved in with Edward and I think this is very unfair. More unfair than Blonc. I said so to Nurse but she said he is getting a big boy now and all she meant is he has stopped doing wee-wees in bed. But I know Edward didn't want him much because it means he has to be very quiet after Johnnie is asleep, but perhaps grown-ups don't care what we think and perhaps they don't know. Not perhaps, but probably.

THE CAMPAIGN AGAINST BLONC

Grannie has started coming down again, always for tea, like she did last year. She is kind but I am a little frightened of her because all her clothes are black. But sometimes she does nice things like letting us dress up in her shawls and her beautiful necklaces. That is, all the girls, and the little boys if they want to. A lot of it is silk in wonderful shining colours; it was what she used to wear before she went black. There is a box of all sorts of lace, creamy, lovely to touch. She wears a lace cap now, but it is black which is not so nice: it makes her hair look extra white.

We found the remains of a crinoline and I thought how difficult to get in. But she says no, she did all sorts of things like the Grand tour, with her husband, who was Papa's father, wearing a tall hat which gentlemen used to wear all the time. They went to Italy and brought back the beautiful marble lady in the middle of the goldfish pond, though I suppose it was Grandpa who paid for it. Grandpa is quite dead.

I am allowed to paddle in the goldfish pond if I don't get my dress wet. It is easier for the boys. They are allowed to swim in the big pond. Herbert swims very well and Edward is trying to catch him up. I am starting to learn to swim but I have to wear a thick swimming costume and I think prickly navy-blue serge is one of the things I don't like most.

So we have not got very far about Blonc. He has

knocked down Margie this time. Margie is Millie and Henry's little sister and she is only just talking properly. I know if it had been Baby who was knocked down Nurse would have made a big fuss, but the cousins have only got a nursery maid with them, because their Nanny is having a holiday, and this girl is frightened of Uncle James so she won't say anything about Blonc. That isn't fair.

Blonc was going to do it again when I was out with Andrew and we were picking up fir-cones, but I yelled and Simon the butler came running out in his green baize apron and he kicked Blonc and Blonc went back into the shrubbery. A silver spoon jumped out of his pocket, which I picked up for him. He said that dog needs confining and he was pleased that I had found the spoon. Confining is a nice word and so is green baize, which sounds like summer. I also think that perhaps we could ask Simon to be on our side in the war against Blonc. He told me about the last dog who was an Irish deer-hound and very handsome but not up to his looks, which was something I didn't quite understand. The dog before that was a poodle. "What a time we had, shaving him!" Simon said. But that was years and years ago.

The boys made an ambush for the cousins' nursery maid; they jumped out of a bush and she screamed. But we know she won't tell Nurse; she is just a cowardy custard, frightened of the boys. But Millie says she loves her. She is supposed to ask the cousins, not of course the big ones, if they have done number-two, but she is frightened to. I always say I have

to Nurse, but sometimes I haven't. But I do not count that as a lie.

Sometimes, when I read fairy tales, even with nice pictures, they are frightening. Poetry is never frightening, even if it is about something true and really sad like the Little Revenge fighting the Spanish, ship after ship all night long and the sailors dying on the decks. Our enemy then was Spain but later it was the Russians and the Indian mutineers and the Boers. And now it is the North-West Frontier, but I don't know where that is, for North is Iceland and West is America. I will ask Aunt Gertie when she comes back.

I hope that will be soon, for we are back to nursery tea and we don't get the scones till they are cold and only thin slices of cake. I wish Mama would hurry up, but Papa is finishing one of those long dull things he writes and she is staying with him. But I think five of us is as important as Papa. She has sent me a picture postcard but that is not much. Still, it goes into my collection. Millie collects picture postcards too; she has an album.

Grannie is sitting in the drawing room most days now. She brings her little black dog, who always makes a dog's nest in the fireplace rug which is so woolly and warm. The dog is called Binky, but I did so like the fireplace rug myself and now I have to share it. Grannie thinks this is a treat for me, but it isn't. She likes Blonc too, and when he comes in he puts his head in her lap and looks up in a gooey sort of way and is good. But there is always someone else

there with him, mostly Uncle James. I can see that Blonc is thinking all the time about chasing us. He knocked Johnnie over again yesterday and would have picked him up, but Nurse stopped him and said he ought to be tied up. Mrs Cook thinks so too; he stole a whole joint which was going to be for Sunday dinner. We had other things instead, the best was baked potatoes and butter. I think I could eat four or five baked potatoes quite easily. Edward said he could eat nine or ten, but I think that is too many for anybody.

Just now I am agreeing with Edward about everything because he has asked Nurse if I can come to the pond and practise swimming with the blow-up cushion and him looking after me. I do so hope she will say yes and not wait till Mama comes. Anyhow I went down to the pond with the boys and sat on a rock beside the place where the water comes twinkling in and there might be fairies riding on the fern leaves, and I watched them swimming. Then Blonc came and jumped in, but they swam round and got hold of his tail, so that he couldn't swim the way he wanted. The boys swim better than he does. But when he came out he shook water all over me and I was afraid he was going to try to pick me up, but I have a big stick. Then I heard Uncle James coming along and shouting for him and he went bouncing away.

There is one very naughty thing Blonc does and that is to chase the sheep. Solly Sticky was very angry about that and no wonder. He went to talk about it to Uncle James, but he came out of the talk feeling

more angry, for I heard him talking to himself about his sheep and that dog. When he was talking to himself he used some bad words. They were worse than I have ever heard and I do not even know how to spell them.

There was an adventure this week, though I was not in it at the beginning, I only guessed that the boys were planning a surprise. What was nice was that Millie and me, but the others are too young, were invited up the big lime tree and when we got to the branch that faces over the garden wall there was a huge bunch of grapes — triumphal was what Edward said, like ancient Rome, and we were each given a small bunch off it. The grapes are the colour that I think Kings' mantles must be. One I peeled and ate the purple peeling and then ate the inside which is a purplefied wet-green and just fits into your mouth so that your tongue can play with it. It is not stealing if we only take one bunch.

There was another boy there, I think he may be a cousin, but I am not sure. I think he is called Peter but I am not even sure about that. He did not say anything to me. But he joined in the conversation. Of course we all talked about Blonc, but Millie and me don't count much with the boys. Herbert — that is Millie's big brother — was very cross because he had

been carving a stick, that is, the head of the stick, and Blonc had run away with it and when Herbert tried to get it back, Blonc broke it. But I do not think Herbert carves well, not like the Indian things Aunt Gertie brought back. But even if it was not much of a carving, we can't have Blonc bullying us.

This evening Mama and Papa have come. Their train was quite late and I was supposed not to be awake, but I could hear the evening train that we can see across three fields, coming grunting up and stopping. Then it goes on, puffing first slow, then quickly, and we hear the carriage coming back from the station and the two horses stamping into the gravel and stopping. Then came the voices and I so wanted Mama to come up. But it was ages and ages before she came and I think I may have cried just a little, but then she did come and she smelled lovely of flowers, not like Nurse, and she cuddled me up and I came before the boys and before Baby, and she gave me a book and it was the new Nesbit which was the book I most wanted, so that I even forgot to tell her about Blonc.

But the next day I didn't see her much because she was doing a lot of grown-up things and sitting beside Granny and showing her some photographs. Nurse was a bit cross and crosser still when Papa came in with a big box of real chocolates to share and Johnnie had the first one, then me. Nurse said — but not directly at Papa but into the air — that it was sure to upset us and we would have to have a grey powder on Saturday. But I hope she will forget. Chocolates

are not poison. Papa said to Nurse that we should have cod liver oil next winter and that is bad enough, though Millie says she quite likes it. But we can have a lemon drop after it.

I think Papa is still writing that book that Mama says will be important and everyone will read it. But I think it will not be a book I will want to read. I am trying to read the new Nesbit very slowly and guess what will be coming next. I had to finish the page and didn't come at once for my bath and so Nurse slapped me, but not hard and I think it was because Papa annoyed her and she always has to say yes to him. Only she put my book onto a high shelf where I cannot reach it. I was almost crying, but I swallowed it.

Anyhow that was all right, because Edward got it down for me; he wants to be next on the list to read it. But I am afraid there will be no magic in this one. It is only about a railway and I don't think I like children as much as the Phoenix and the Carpet ones, who were more like us. So then Edward said to me to come to the pond in the afternoon and I would get a surprise. I am allowed to go to the pond alone if there is someone else there. On the way there I have found some lovely flat stones with moss like what I think is meant by an unending vista, for you can think of the moss being forests and I put in the tiniest flowers I can find.

Also, Mrs Cook is making a huge cake for Mama. I went to look and she gave me a cherry and let me

lick the cream spoon. She said how Mama had been a harum-scarum but now she had grown up to be a lovely lady. I do wonder what she was before she grew up. Was she like me?

So I went to the pond and there were the boys, as well as this new Peter who has reddish hair and I think he is some kind of a cousin. Herbert had a stick and Blonc first tried to get it and, when Herbert snatched it away, tried to catch hold of Herbert's swimsuit which is only like short trousers. But Herbert and Edward and the new boy all pushed Blonc's head under the water. They did not drown him, but he got all choky and rushed back to the bank and he had his tail between his legs, which means that he is frightened. They said perhaps they had frightened him enough, but in quite a short time he seemed as bad as ever, though he did not go back into the water. Instead he stood on the edge and barked.

Aunt Gertie has come back so I hope we shall soon be getting drawing room tea again, though I am not sure if the boys want it as much as I do. They don't like having to have good manners, but I don't mind. It is easy to say please. But almost at once Aunt Gertie had an argument with Uncle James. Now, she is Granny's daughter, just like Mama is her daughter and there is an uncle who lives far, far away in Australia and who sent back some seeds of australian trees and one of them is growing. Sometimes I stroke its leaves to encourage it. But Uncle James is Granny's a lot younger brother, that is, what he calls the Older Generation. So he thinks the older generation is

always right, but that can't be true or there would be no history. He also says he is taking the place of Grandpapa, but Grannie laughs at him sometimes and says, "Come, come, Jim" which sounds funny, but means that Grannie is not going to let him be right over everything. And I think, myself, that Grannie is more pleased with Aunt Gertie who is her daughter, than with her brother. I think Grannie understands that Uncle James rather likes bullying people. He can never bully Papa because Papa always ends by laughing and saying something clever. And mostly Papa is on Aunt Gertie's side, though he teases her a little too. I think this is part of what families are about.

Anyway, people like different things. Aunt Gertie has a very friendly cat called Smiles after the cat in Alice. but I do think some of the Alice pictures are very frightening, though I know some of the Alice poetry by heart. Once I said some in class and Miss Stevenson said if I could remember that I would be able to remember anything.

Mrs Cook looks after Aunt Gertie's cat when she is away, but he purrs and gets on Aunt Gertie's knee as soon as she comes back.

It is difficult to understand what is the quarrel, but I think Aunt Gertie has been doing something that Uncle James does not like. I heard him say stupid things about Aunt Gertie's travels, which are so interesting. Also I heard a little scrap between Mrs Cook and Nurse which made me think that Aunt

Gertie didn't want to marry someone who was a friend of Uncle James. I think she was right. We should only marry people we like. I remember once some grown-ups were talking about Papa, and Mama said I rushed into his arms, which you wouldn't do unless you like someone a lot.

I do wonder that Uncle James is not married. He is the one who smokes big cigars. My Papa smokes too, but not such big ones and only does it when he is writing his book. There is a smoking room in the house where ladies don't go much. It smells all the time and there are some books which only grown-ups are allowed to read. I asked Papa about them and he said they had some stupid and ugly pictures and he can't see why Uncle James keeps them, which just shows that grown-ups don't always agree.

Something very interesting happened but nothing to do with the rest of us, or Blonc. Aunt Gertie came out of the drawing room with her face red and tied-up looking, like it always gets when Uncle James teases her, for that is what he does, just like the boys sometimes tease me. And she said to me come here and took my hand hard and I walked with her to the garden seat and she began to tell me about Votes for Women and this is very important. I had heard of

this, but just as words, so I did not really understand, though now I do. When Aunt Gertie explained I knew it was right and that the way things are managed now is just like the boys telling me where to hide or even where to hold on if we are climbing and we might have found a better way ourselves. It is useful to be told, but it is nicer to do it for yourself. We just got used to the boys knowing better and that is silly.

So I almost at once agreed with Aunt Gertie, though I am not quite sure what Members of Parliament really do and why voting for them matters so much. Because anyhow there is King Edward the Seventh at the top and that is that. But then, there was Queen Victoria and Queen Elizabeth who won the war with Spain. I said were all the Members of Parliament men? And she said yes, but not for ever, which I thought sounded exciting.

She told me a lot more, about poor women who have to sew all day and only get pennies at the end and the men in Parliament don't help them. She went on and on and sometimes not seeing that I felt muddled and I could see how she wanted to hit Uncle James who had laughed at her, and it was interesting to see that grown-ups can hurt one another and want to hurt one another, and it is nothing to do with wars. Later, when I was in bed and Mama came to tuck me in like she mostly does unless there is a grown-up party, I asked about Votes for Women, and Mama laughed and said politics were very dull and better left to men, and about the poor women who have to

sew or make matches, she said, well, there are always poor people and often it was their own fault because when they had money they spent it on drink.

So I am not quite sure about it all and which side I am, but I know I like Aunt Gertie much, much more than I like Uncle James. In fact, I think I don't like Uncle James at all and once I saw Lizzie, the under-housemaid, crying and when I asked she said it was something Uncle James had said, but she wouldn't tell me what. And this was the same day that Blonc chased the sheep and one of them got stuck in the fence and broke its leg and Solly Sticky is now very angry indeed. So Uncle James gave him the cost of the sheep, but he looked just as angry when he walked out. I tried to say I was sorry but he didn't seem to hear. And I think perhaps we have eaten part of the sheep, though it seems different when it is called mutton and sometimes I wish we did not have to eat animals. But I do like chicken. That is my best treat and for my birthday I always have roast chicken and baked apples with cream. Nurse is always cross about this and of course Christmas pudding, and mostly I have to have at least one grey powder that evening. She is the same about Johnnie, but she cannot make Edward take anything unless he is really sick or after measles, and there is a real doctor to say what we are to eat, and often this is jelly and that is nice.

I do like the doctor at home who comes when we are ill. He gave Mama a lovely cool thing to put on my spots when Johnnie and I had measles and

Johnnie had to wear little gloves to stop him from scratching at the sore bits. Chickenpox is not as bad as measles, but whooping cough is the worst and we have to have them all, but afterwards we went up to the sea and rode on donkeys. But I was not allowed to read for a month because of my eyes and Nurse does not like reading aloud. Anyhow she does not read well. Mama reads better, but she does not like reading my sort of books. Aunt Gertie reads aloud best and stops to show us the pictures when there are some. Last year Edward and I both had winter coughs which are horrid because they go on and on. But the doctor gave us heroin lozenges after the coughs had been going on for ages: they stopped the coughs much better than black currant, though they did not taste so nice. I remember that because I said to myself that now I am a heroine like Boadicea.

Mama is very good when we are ill, much nicer than Nurse; she played finger games with us. But now she is more fond of Baby and this time, as soon as she came she began to think about Baby. I know she came to me first, but when she had tucked me up I could hear her picking up Baby and not listening to Nurse who was trying to interrupt and Baby was almost asleep but Mama purred over him and it sounded as if Nurse had been cross. Of course, I was not in it, only the door to the other room was open, but it did make Nurse cross the next morning. I think Baby is not very interesting so far, and he has broken some of Johnnie's toys, though mostly ones that Johnnie is tired of, but I expect he will be worth having when he talks properly and can do things with us.

In a way I would like to talk to Mama about our war with Blonc, but in another way, not. It is our private war and she might start telling us what to do, or she might take the side of Uncle James and say we were not to have Blonc as our enemy. But I don't really think she would do that because of Blonc being a tyrant and she says we must always be against tyrants. Only foreign countries have them.

One nice thing has been that the boys let me help them on the great rat hunt, which happens every year when we stay with Grannie. There are empty old rooms at the top of the house with a few crumbly bits of cupboards and chairs and old rugs piled up in the corners. The rats get in there, so we get two of the farm dogs who are terriers. They hunt out the rats and we all shout and try to hit them. Herbert hit Edward by accident, but Edward did not mind at all although he had a huge bruise afterwards. The other boy, Peter, did not really like it and I am not sure how much I really like it, but hunting them out is exciting, though all the time, when one of them escapes, I am glad for him too because even rats must want not to die. Sometimes I make up an If I was a Rat story, but not while we are hunting and I am one of the boys. We try to kill more rats than last year. Blonc is no good at rat hunting and gets into the way and gets accidentally hit. Even if he found a rat under his nose he would not know how to kill it as the farm terriers do.

At last they let me take Johnnie up the hill, though he did not like it so much as I wanted him to. He did like seeing the rabbits and there were some butterflies on the tall, yellow flowers, but he did not really like the tiny pansies as much as I do. I never pick them because they belong to the fairies. I know the fairies are not real, but I think that does not matter.

When we came back — and I brought her a bunch of flowers — Grannie said I was a good girl like my Aunt Gertrude. I did not know before that her real name ended with rude. If you think it like that it is funny and so are a lot of names. So I have just seen that words can be taken to bits and when you put them together again they are something else, like primrose and if you take it to bits it is a very, very tidy girl called Rose. And lion is a sofa and eatable is eat a bull. This is one of the best games to play by oneself, but perhaps I will tell Millie. Not the boys.

Sometimes the boys are rude, and we are always being told not to be rude, or that one of the others are rude. But what is it really? I think Aunt Gertie is really, really rude to Uncle James. But it is all his fault. I was listening at lunch to Aunt Gertie being rude to Uncle James, but without his really knowing it. It was in the way she said some words. It is all his fault anyhow. Mama had brought me down with her so that I was having grown-up lunch instead of nursery

dinner. Lunch has things like slices of meat with little bits of parsley sitting on them and cheese which Nurse says is bad for me, but Mama lets me have it. Also they drink wine. Papa gave me a sip once but it tastes like medicine.

Then I went to the pond, but it was not such fun as I had hoped because Nurse came and took me in and out of my bathing dress and rubbed me very hard. But the boys did help me to swim and said I would soon be able to do it on my own. After that Blonc came down with Uncle James, who threw a stick into the water. Blonc jumped in and picked it up and shook himself so that there was water in all the ferns which look sparkly and nice. Then he did it again but the third time the boys caught Blonc and pulled him about in the water until Uncle James shouted at them. When they came out he scolded them about doing things to dumb animals. But I think Blonc is not dumb at all, he knows everything that is going on and turns it his way, and for instance he ate the special bits that were being kept for Grannie's little drawing room dog. And he has tried to make up to Peter, the boy who is staying, and Peter is beginning to be a little on his side. Agnes says Peter is a cousin twice removed. But what is he removed from?

Now the boys are making a house right up one of the big trees, so Millie and I started another one and we let Henry and Johnnie help us because we are kind, and they were quite good at bringing us things. Johnnie even brought us the hall string that the

grown-ups keep for parcels and important things and we are not supposed to take, but I took about an arm length of string from inside, which is the proper way of taking string and told him to take the rest back. After that we went into the vegetable garden, shutting the gate carefully in case Peter Rabbit comes in, and Big Jock who is the head gardener gave us a huge shiny leaf of raspberries and when we said thank you he gave us two lovely plums, so ripe that their purple coats were breaking. We ate them at once but let Henry and Johnnie have some raspberries. There is another gardener but he is not so nice and does not tell us the names of flowers like Big Jock does. Aunt Gertie does the rose garden; the roses all have Latin names and I think they are first declension. Everyone says that Grannie used to be good at gardening, but now she is too old. It must be horrible to be old.

Blonc has now done his old, bad thing. He pushed over little Maggie, Millie's baby sister who is only a little older than my Baby, and then picked her up by the back of her frock and carried her over, wagging his great stupid tail, to Uncle James. Luckily Aunt Gertie was there too and picked up Maggie and gave her one of the grown-up sweeties which are very nice. Uncle James scolded Blonc, but really he thought it was funny and Blonc went on wagging his tail which he would not have done if it had been a real scolding, and really he thought it was funny, Uncle James I mean, and I cannot bear it when grown-ups think that something is funny which isn't at all funny to us, and Maggie was crying and had to have her frock

changed. Of course she wasn't really hurt, but I expect she thought she was and she went on crying. I just wished I could cut off Blonc's great wagging tail.

Agnes helped us a bit with our tree house. She can reach right up and climb as well as the boys though she does not come climbing very often. She is cross because Mama wants her to wear stays which are the grown-up kind of ordinary bodice, like my knickers are buttoned onto. But stays are tight because they are made out of whale bones. I had never before thought of whether whales had bones or fins. They do sound very uncomfortable, so why should Agnes have to wear them? Millie says that Ursula wears stays when she sometimes comes down for late dinner and they are very uncomfortable, but Ursula has a lovely dress, all silk and lace and just little cuffs for sleeves, so it may be worth it. But she is almost two years older than Agnes and I know that she has danced with almost grown-up boys, so perhaps she thinks it worth while. I suppose that if Mama gave Agnes a really beautiful dress like the fairy godmother gave Cinderella, she might not mind wearing stays.

Today we had what the grown-ups think is a treat, but I don't think it is, nor do the boys really. We went over to the house which is called something park, but it isn't like a park in a town. It is a bigger house than Grannie's but not very much. Only the boys, who went there on their bicycles, had a really good time, because the Park boys have a lovely railway in a room at the back which they have for themselves. But it

was not much fun for me or Millie, or even Henry and Johnnie, because Nurse came with us in the pony-cart and she would not let me drive at all, although Aunt Gertie lets me and really the pony knows all about the road. We did meet a motor car coming the other way and we shouted Stinker at it, though I don't think they heard. The worst was, we had nursery dinner there instead of grown-up lunch and it was mutton stew with carrots which I don't like and rice pudding and only one chocolate each although we were guests. The children there are two girls and a baby boy, but also there are the big boys who have the railway, and that was what I wanted to see because Edward had told me about it.

But Nurse and their nurse, who was very old, at least I thought so, and she shuffled about like an old hen, talked and talked and the children did not seem to like us much. I so wanted to see the railway and so did Millie. But their Nurse said I was too young to appreciate it. I hate being young. I am not young really. Seven years old is not young. And the boys enjoyed themselves and came back with things they had printed in a kind of stamping machine that the Park boys had. It was just not fair. The only nice thing was their dog. He is almost as tall as Blonc but even his shape is different. He is some sort of hound, with very long legs and gentle eyes. He looks as if he had come out of a drawing by someone very clever. I don't think those people deserve such a nice dog.

I have nearly finished my Nesbit book I have been reading. I had meant to make it stretch and I went back and read my best bits twice, but even so I am near the end. Then I will let Millie read it before Edward, although Millie reads slower than me, but I have kept on telling her about it every morning. I don't like the Sunday books so much, though it is exciting when Christian has all those adventures in Pilgrim's Progress and I do like the picture of Vanity Fair.

Uncle James came in when I was reading it in a corner of the hall and said "I see you're reading Piggy-poggy". I thought that was not a polite way of speaking about a book like that which is meant to make people better, though I don't really see how it does. Aunt Gertie had brought a book about Indian religions which is counted as a Sunday book, but it is quite exciting and full of animals and battles, though the names are rather difficult.

Millie and I go to church if Grannie is going in the victoria, but she does not go much because it is hard on the coachman. Instead she reads bits of the Bible herself and gets Aunt Gertie to play some hymn tunes on the piano in the drawing room. They are often rather sad tunes. Mama sometimes plays very nice ones, but she says that Uncle James has let the piano go out of tune. Sometimes I try to understand what

the music signs mean, but it is rather difficult. Perhaps I shall get Aunt Gertie or even Mama to explain. I heard Papa talking to Uncle James about getting a car. Grannie does not like the idea, and it would mean an engineer to drive it. But it would be very exciting. I have been in a motor car several times myself, but I don't like sitting on people's knees, even Mama's and being held. Of course the boys want it; they think they will be able to learn to drive it. I just wonder.

The boys and the big girls walk to church but it is quite a long way, though it is nice in summer when all the hedges are in flower. If we go we have to sit very still and listen to the sermon. Sometimes when the others come back they are making jokes about the sermon, and so does Uncle James. But Grannie never does. The grown-ups have easy meals on Sunday, so that there is very little washing up and Simon goes for a long walk. I saw him once coming back; he had no hat and no tie either, so that he looked not at all Sundayish. Once he brought us back a whole bag full of berries from the blackthorns which are like little plums. He said they could be made into wine.

When we were talking about church, Millie said that if we prayed hard enough we might be able to turn Blonc into a good dog. That would be a miracle. I know miracles happen but I don't think this is the kind that would count. I just can't see Blonc paying any attention. She said what if an angel would come down and tell him to be a good dog? I said well, all he would do would be to say silly old angel. And perhaps bite her. Millie said she didn't think angels

could be bitten and even if they were it would not hurt them. But this is something we can't really know.

I am still thinking about Votes for Women and about what Aunt Gertie has told me about when she was a girl and did not go to a proper school, but there was an old friend of Grannie who used to come and stay and help her after Grandpa died, which of course old people do, but he was not so very old. Uncle James was away at College and anyhow although he is Grannie's brother, he was only the younger brother then. There was another brother who died of some illness. I think perhaps he was Peter's grandpapa. So this old friend, who was a Professor, came to help, and he taught Aunt Gertie who was still a girl, as much as a school could have made her learn. It was mostly history and also about pictures and china, so now she can pick up a little bowl and tell at once where it comes from. I saw her do this once when she came to stay with us and Mama took her to visit some friends who have lots and lots of china, some nice but some very boring and you must take great care if you even touch it. But they listened very carefully to what Aunt Gertie said, which was nice. So now Aunt Gertie knows a lot about china and about how it is made, and that made her interested in the people who made and painted the china, and somehow she even began writing about it. But not stories, only just what they did to make it, and that, she says, is a kind of history and a kind of geography too.

So I think Votes for Women is partly finding out

about other people and about things you are not taught at school. And I think some of the things the boys are learning at school do not amount to much. But I would like to play football only Mama says no girls ever play football or ever will. It is a rough game. But some girls play hockey, I know, only Mama says it is really a rough game too and they wear very short skirts and sometimes the balls fly up and hit them, and you might have your nose broken, which would make you ugly for life.

Blonc did something new. The grown-up newspapers are always put tidily onto the big round table in the hall, beside the big pot with the palm tree which never seems to grow. Blonc pulled the papers off and ran away with them and they came to pieces and got scattered all over the front lawn. He had never done this before, but I suppose he was bored. In a way I was a little on his side because the newspapers are not interesting and they often make people quarrel, I mean of course the grown-ups. I have looked at them sometimes, but they are not at all interesting and sometimes the lines get all squidged together, and there is only one paper that ever has any pictures and these are mostly of people who are not really interesting. So Blonc had his nose stuck into the papers and Uncle James beat him. But I don't think he can have minded much because only ten minutes after, he was prancing about and snatching the bits of wood that the boys were going to make a cricket wicket with. I think cricket-wicket sounds nice and jongly. You could say wicked-cricket-wicket-

hit-it. I love making funny words; Edward is very good at that, if I can get him to start, but sometimes he says it is childish.

This was a day I shall always remember. I had wanted to go to the old plantation with the boys. I knew I could climb the easy tree, which is an old spruce which was left when the rest were cut, and it has almost a staircase up it. So I wanted to try another and so did Millie, who is climbing much better than she used to. I thought I could go perhaps with Millie, and anyhow with the two little boys who are quite sensible. But the boys said they knew we couldn't and they were going further up the hill and perhaps down the other side. And I must stay with Millie, who they know doesn't want to climb as much as I do, and in the end that meant staying with Nurse and the nursemaid who has come with Millie and the two babies as well. So that was spoiling everything. I had so wanted to show Millie and the two little boys how well I climbed. But it turned out different.

So there was Nurse with Baby in his pushcart and Johnnie, whom she kept on holding, though he was always wriggling his hand away, and then there was Millie with the little nursemaid who always kept dropping behind because she had little Margaret in

another pushcart. Henry was with us; he and Johnnie were talking nonsense to one another, at least it sounded like that, but it may have been a game. Their nursemaid had little Maggie's hand, but didn't say a word to anyone else.

We came out past the pig sty and I gave Mrs Pig a crust I had been keeping specially for her. Then Blonc came bounding out and Nurse said "Oh drat, we shall have to take the dog with us. I wish they would control him". She does not really like Blonc any more than we do. And then we started along the Ride, which has sheep on both sides behind the railings. I kept thinking that if Millie's nurse had been there, the two nurses would be gabble-gobbling to one another the whole time, but our Nurse looks down on the nursemaid who is quite young and scared of her.

All the sheep on one side were wethers and on the other side they were ewes and a ram. The rams have huge horns like Little Boy Blue had, and they do what is nearly shouting. They stamp their feet, too. We hadn't gone far when Blonc began barking at the sheep. The big ram seemed to be shouting back and stamped his hoofs hard. Nurse said "We'd better go back and take that dog away." She always calls Blonc THAT DOG. "Always going for the poor sheep" she said. The ram was now very angry and I wanted to watch, for it was really funny, but Nurse was turning the pushcart and the nursemaid hit Blonc with a stick, but the stick broke and Blonc didn't even notice.

Then all at once Blonc was right over the fence and

THE CAMPAIGN AGAINST BLONC

rushing at the sheep and the ram rushed at him with his head down and the next minute he was rolling on the ground and the ram was shouting and stamping because he had won, and the sheep all jostled together and both our babies began to cry as Nurse hurried the pushcart away and Johnnie and Henry ran to the fence to look, and then Millie and I ran after them in case they managed to get into the field, and we could see Blonc rolling over and howling. And then the next minute he was running away on three legs and the ram stood there shouting. It was just like a person shouting and I could see what the words could have been, how he had won his battle and saved his flock from the enemy and everything was wonderful. I felt myself kind of on his side, wanting to jump to the moon and shout.

But Nurse was rushing back to the house and Baby was crying and Millie was trying to catch Henry and the nursemaid was almost crying and Johnnie was hanging onto the fence and jumping his feet because he was so excited. I told him to run after us, but I thought I had better run and catch up with the babies. And there was Blonc ahead of us rushing into the house, his tail between his legs and a smudge of red on one side. Then there were the grown-ups all round him, trying to see if he was really hurt, but they decided it was only a light cut and a nasty bruise, and they were all in the hall looking after Blonc, even my Papa who isn't really interested in animals.

Little Maggie began to cry and nursemaid was no good, so I gave Maggie one of the big front garden

flowers which are special and we are supposed not to pick them, but this was a special time so it was all right and Maggie stopped crying. Nurse hadn't seen properly what had happened, but I had and I told it very well and how Blonc was always going for the sheep and how he had got what he deserved. But Uncle James did not think of it that way, or did not like to, and began saying that Solly Sticky would have to get rid of that ram, which was a danger. "The brute could be a danger to the children" said Uncle James, but I thought he doesn't really like the children and he is using us as an excuse in his war with Solly.

So I said "Uncle James, the ram is not dangerous to us," and I could hear that I was talking loud, so I had to go on and I said: "Blonc is more dangerous. He knocks us down," and then my Papa laughed and so did Grannie who has a funny little tinkly laugh. Then all the grown-ups began talking and Blonc kissed Uncle James' hand. He had a cut under one leg, but by now it was only bleeding a little bit and they put some stuff on it. If he had been really hurt he could not have run so fast.

So I said to Aunt Gertie: "The ram was defending his flock from their enemy." I know the word flock was a good word to use because it has a sort of extra meaning like Bible words sometimes have. "He was truly a hero," I said.

Then Aunt Gertie said: "Like Perseus," and I said: "So Blonc is the gorgon," because I had read all about this in the Kingsley book with the Greek stories, but some are very sad.

They all laughed, but Blonc had settled down almost under Uncle James and sometimes Uncle James reached down and patted him and he licked Uncles James' hand and I was almost sorry for him. Then Grannie said "If this is a dangerous ram, we should keep the dear children away from the farm." I couldn't help it, I said "No, no, Grannie it is Blonc who is dangerous." And then Grannie laughed again and her face wrinkled up and she said "But none of the family are frightened, are we?" So all of us jumped about saying no, no, no, especially Maggie who just couldn't stop.

Johnnie had hung onto the fence and watched the sheep when it was over, and the ram was in among the ewes and I thought he ought not to say what he had seen them doing. I have been explained to about how animals get married, and of course with a farm it is like hundreds of wives, but the rams do not look after their wives, not at all. They just get on top of them.

I liked it all best when the boys came back and we told them what had happened and I did most of the telling. And there was Blonc in a corner with Uncle James only patting him now and then, and the rest of us whispering, inventing new names for him that meant he was never-ever going to be king of the castle again. I wondered if he understood what we said. I suppose not, but I am sure he now knew that he had been beaten by one of the sheep. He had lost his battle for ever.

We could stop thinking about him too, because he was kept in for quite a long time and we didn't have to watch in case he came out and bounced at us again. Millie and I went along the ride between the two fields by ourselves without Nurse, and we called over to the ram that he had won the great battle, and he lifted his head with those great curly horns and looked at us. I could see he was very proud. Solly Sticky had heard about it and he grinned at us when we went by with a barrow of turnips. We said "Good Afternoon" but it was the ram we had to talk to. I stood on the bottom wire so that I was high up and I shouted to the ram: "The Tyranny is over." That was our words that we said very loudly; Millie said them too. I like these words. I chose them myself.

COLD IN COVENTRY

Jessie Kesson

EMMA KNEW THE ADMITTANCE room well. Years of polishing its every nook and cranny had forged an intimacy between herself and The Room.

Fourteen now, she had been eight when Madam Superintendent of the Training Institution for Destitute Girls had put her under the charge of an older girl who had 'instructed' her in what was to become her Specific Weekly Task... the 'Thoroughing Out' of the Admittance Room. Once a week, for seven years, she had 'Turned out' this room. She found herself counting the times... Fifty two weeks in a year... Seven times fifty-two...three hundred and sixty four times...

The room hadn't changed, she thought, gazing round it. But then it didn't have long enough to change. She had been away from it for only three months in her...'First Situation'.

Days though, rising up in her memory of those seven years, when the Room took on a more ominous title and became the Re-Admission Room. She had never known it — until now — in *that* guise, but had shared with fifty other girls in the Institution, avid speculation on what happened to a girl returned In Disgrace to a Room which could so swiftly change its

name and its purpose.

The Summonsing Bell for Morning Prayers clanged through her thoughts. It would be followed by girls rushing past her door and along the corridor to Chapel... If she was blind, if she had to stay forever in this room she would never be lonely. Not as long as hearing lasted and she could hear the Summonsing Bells ring out the Divisions of each days duties.

Listening to the sounds of the girls approaching footsteps she knew that they wouldn't open the door of the Room. They would halt outside it. She knew that too. To savour for a brief moment the relief of being on the *right* side of safety.

Pray for Peter
Pray for Paul.

She mocked after their disappearing backs.

Never pray for ME at all!!!

The small gesture of defiance smiled her. Closing the door quietly the sound of singing Morning Prayers rose faintly from the distance. She had no need to hear its *words*. She knew them. Taking up the Prayer itself, she sang it as if she was still amongst them in the Chapel...

Father of all we bow to Thee
Who dwellest in Heaven adored
Forever hallowed by Thy Name
By all beneath the skies
From day to day we humbly own
The hand that feeds us still
Our sins before Thee we confess

O may they be forgiven...

Emmas's sin would not be forgiven. At least not by Madam. The reason for her dismissal from her job had arrived before herself. To be read out by Madam...

Kingston Manor
Wivesfeld
Sussex   10 April 1895

My Cook informs me that Emma Gartly was a pleasant girl to have in the kitchen, but her mind was seldom on her duties. As she is the **Second** *Girl I have employed from your institution whose work has now proved unsatisfactory, I have no option but to withdraw my Patronage.*

...The loss of a Patron... *That* Emma knew would be unforgivable.

'Do you *agree* with the *Reason* for your dismissal?' Madam had asked.

'Yes Madam'.

'Have you anything... to say for yourself?'

'No Madam.'

...Plenty to say. But there were no words that would justify her failure to Madam. Maybe, she thought, trying to clarify it in her *own* mind ...Maybe if she had been a tablemaid... she had fancied being a tablemaid after seeing photographs of former girls in their

uniforms. Smart, tablemaids had looked. White streamers hanging down from the crowns of their caps to their shoulders... Or even an Under Housemaid... Clean in their white all-embracing aprons... But — scullerymaid — Emma had felt so dirty all the time — A dirty, greasy girl — Bent always over a wooden sink. Half-hidden inside a big oilskin apron. Or down on her knees in a bag apron scrubbing the stone flags of the Kitchen floor. Everybody rushing past her as if they hadn't seen her... As if she didn't exist. Flinging everything that was dirty into a sink that seldom seemed to be empty. In the three months in her Situation she had felt caught up in a whirl of Apology... Bent under a perpetual Vow of Atonement.

...*Sorry*, Cook. I didn't know you wanted ME to *chop* the Parsley... I'll do it straight away...

...I thought I *had* taken *all* the eyes out of the potatoes... I'll go over them again... Won't take me a minute'...

...The Cod's Heads ...I gave them to the Cat.. I didn't *know* you wanted them for the staffs' fish soup...

...No Cook... I wouldn't want THAT... I'd *never* want the CAT to choke on the Cod's heads... I... *like* the CAT... I'll remember next time...

Cook was right in her warnings... "You'd better *had* remember my Girl!" Right too in her forecast that Emma "Hadn't the Makings of a scullerymaid"... No wonder Cook "didn't know what was to become of her".. Emma didn't know herself...

She had been shying away from speculation on Madam's ultimate decision on her fate. Warily touching the alternatives rising to the surface of her mind.

... It wouldn't be to the Workhouse... you had to be Pregnant to be sent to the Workhouse... the Reformatory... She hadn't been Bad enough for the Reformatory. If she'd been a Boy. From the Boys' Division, it could have been a Training Ship. Or away on some other ship to work on a farm in Canada. Options for the Boys' in Disgrace opened wide horizons in her mind. Sea and space. Time to recover yourself on a long voyage to Destination and Doom. Maybe... maybe they wouldn't bother taking you back In Disgrace... all the way from Canada... A further Period of Training... Madam might decide on *that*. Not *here* though. You'd be Out In The World as Madam described it. She didn't want the other girls to be 'influenced' by what you'd discovered Out In The World.

As in other critical moments of her short life Emma began to manipulate Time. Caught up in a warp of her own making. Clutching briefly at remembered safety.... Just three short months ago she was — safe — in this Room. Cleaning it out. In a day that was Ordinary. The Room itself hadn't changed. The huge Tract on the wall above the marble mantel. Signed by St Paul, it still exhorted all who set eyes on it... Little Children Love Ye One Another... It was the change in *her* circumstances that altered her attitude towards it. St Paul had got it wrong. Had come to the wrong address. The girls had never "loved" one another.

Self-preservation had prevented it. *Madam's* approval was ALL. They would have shot their grandmother's if such a dastardly deed would have won them Madam's Approval.

The Breakfast Bell ringing out brought speculation to an end. Prepared this time for the rush of girls pausing and passing the door of the Room, Emma was ready to Pounce. To deprive them of smugness. Flinging open the door to confront them:

...Look at me...Take a *Good* look. I haven't turned into a Monster.

Taken by surprise they scattered. Scuttling past the door. I'm NOT.. she called after them... I'm Not PREGNANT..... You Lousy LOT...

Still, she had to admit to herself when her brief feeling of Derring Do had faded, she herself had acted exactly the same on the day any girl sacked from her job, returned In Disgrace... A Day that became High Lit. Lifting them all up out of the monotonous routine of ordinary days. The girl's failure making the others feel... 'The Good Ones'... A rare feeling. One to be savoured. Closing ranks. Making excuses to run round to the laundry past the window of the Room to get a quick peek at the girl inside it. Feeling she must have changed. Must carry the imprint of failure on her face.

Times though... times slipping into mind when Emma had been in high favour with the other girls.

At night — that safest time — in their small, black iron beds, the 'covering' defences of the day cast off, set aside with their Combinations and Liberty Bodices.

...Tell us a story, Emma...

Their pleas rising up in her mind.

...A poem Emma... A poem from the Book...

The sources of her Stories still stood intact in the large, mahogany Bookcase... Fingering through them...

Jessica's First Prayer. Christy's Old Organ. Eric. Little By Little. Saturday's Child...

All stories which implied that it was better to die young and Saved, than to grow old and become a Sinner, which Madam sometimes seemed to think they had signs of becoming.

...A sad Poem, Emma... The Orphan Boy...

...I'll let *You* dry next time we're on Washing Up if you say The Orphan Boy...

Strange, Emma thought, putting Poems of Victorian Childhood back in its place in the Bookcase. Its shiny leather cover still slippery to her touch. Strange, the girls seldom wept for themselves. But often shed tears for a boy in a book.

... They *couldn't* have forgotten... They could *never* have forgotten *That*...

They *had* forgotten. Emma recognised that the moment Agnes Bradley opened the door of the Room. Facing each other in a second's silence that spanned

a decade of shared childhood with no acknow-ledgement of former allegiance. That hurt. It hurt more than *Madam* could. And Madam *knew* it. A girl was officially appointed on a Day like this, as her Go Between...

"INVENTORY" Agnes set the Form down on the table. "Madam has checked your trunk." In her official role Agnes's voice had taken on the sound of Madam... "One Morning Cap Missing. One apron beyond reasonable repair." It was only when Agnes reached the door that she sounded like Agnes. Known of old...

"*You'll* have some *Explaining* to do... It better be good."

Missing Cap. Torn apron... Wear and Tear? Not a good enough reason. Emma hadn't been long enough away from the Institution to claim for Wear and Tear. The Truth? Emma grappled for words that could contain the *Truth*.

...It was the Boot Boy, Madam. Always on the look-out for me in his shed behind the Kitchen Garden, when I'd run out for more parsley and spring onions and things. He grabbed me from behind one day. Pinched my cap and wouldn't give it back unless I gave him a Kiss...

The very thought of Madam's reaction to a *Kiss*, and a Boy — Boot or otherwise, flung Truth straight out of the windows of Emma's mind. Though truth it was. There had been no relationship on *Emma's* part with the Boot Boy. *COOK* would never have stood

for That... She didn't like the Boot Boy.... "*Another* of her Ladyship's Charitables" she said of him. "From that Barnardo's"... Cook couldn't forgive him for not wiping his boots properly on the Scraper at the Back Door..."dragging all the Dirt into my Kitchen" she complained.

Once Emma remembered, having *herself* discovered something about the deficiency of the Boot Scraper... Only once had she had a sudden impulse to speak up in defence of the Boot Boy ...It's his Boots, Cook... Like *my* Boots. Too big for the Scraper... They don't take a right Grip. They just slide along it...

Emma had not yet been exhorted to... Beware of Pity... Nor had she lived long enough yet to think that the *real* danger lay in NOT... having pity... So. Mindful of Cook's feelings towards the Boot Boy, as sole Counsel For The Defence Emma had kept silent about the Scraper.

"My Cap got lost in the Laundry, Madam," she would say to Madam. "Things were always getting lost or torn there." The lie would be more acceptable than the truth. No *wonder* Madam often accused them of lying. They *were* liars... Of a kind... They needed something, somebody to boast about... The kind of parents they would *liked* to have had. The homes they would like to have lived in. Emma didn't suppose for a *minute* that the girls believed *her* claim to having been "Born in a *Big* House". Though it was true... as far as it went... She simply omitted to mention that it

COLD IN COVENTRY

was the Workhouse. They accepted each others' lies. They had need of them.

> *O give thanks*
> *O give thanks*
> *O give thanks unto the Lord*
> *For He is gracious and His mercy*
> *Endureth*
> *Endureth forever...*

The girls voices sounding up from Chapel brought Breakfast to an end. Bringing to her mind their *own* version

> *There is a happy land*
> *Far far away*
> *Where we get bread and marg*
> *Three times a day*
> *Ham and eggs we never see*
> *Nor sugar in our tea*
> *And we are gradually*
> *Fading away...*

For the first time since she had entered the Room Emma felt the pain of Outwithness as the girls rushed laughing past the door for recreation in the walled Bleaching Green. Free to themselves to be at one with each other. Full of shared secrecies. Flinging themselves down on their backs. Their long, black stockinged legs scything the air. Convulsed with laughter as they chorused a song of Protest against the rigidity of their days.

...HOLY MOSES
I am dying
Just a word before I go
Put the cat up on the table
Put the Poker up its HOL...Y MOSES...

"...Your Breakfast," Agnes announced, clamping down the tray before distancing herself from the table... "AND... Madam will see you in her Office at ten o'clock."

"I'm not hungry," Emma slid the tray along the table. "I don't want Breakfast."

"That's up to YOU" Agnes shrugged. "You *know* the Rules. They haven't changed. No dinner till you've eaten your Breakfast."

Mindful of how food was so often on their minds and Madam's puzzled claim that she... 'could find no bottom to their hunger,' Emma decided that her recently acquired knowledge of Food — Out In The World — could not fail to 'rattle' Agnes...

"I have NEVER been hungry since I left *here*," she claimed, with truth on her side.

"Cook gave me plenty of Tastes. She said I needed 'Feeding Up'. I got left-overs from Upstairs. And Seconds when there was any left... AND... I *always* got to scrape the Cake Mixture from the bottom of her Baking Bowl!"

"Is... THAT?" Agnes asked when she reached the door. "Is... THAT... why you've got FAT!"

"I'm NOT," Emma shouted before Agnes could reach the end of the Corridor, "I'm not Pregnant. I

got PLENTY of CHANCES!"

Chances. *That* would slay Agnes. It would kill her. Emma stood relishing her small moment of triumph.

Chances...whispered about. Speculated upon. Anticipated for that Out In The World time which beckoned them all. The clothes they'd choose for themselves. Frocks that didn't have to last till that long time when you..."*grew* into them"... Dances... Boys... Not Pregnancy itself. Never Pregnancy... You *knew* what would happen if you were Pregnant. But ... the Preludes to Pregnancy. Ah... *That* was a different thing... being in love... A state much discussed. Deeply desired... *CHANCES!!!*

It was on the long walk to Madam's Office, that Emma, walking several paces behind Agnes as her lack of status now required, took an old escape route into the realms of prayer and fantasy...

...Dear God make be Back On A Visit... All Dressed-Up Head Housemaid. With a photo of me in my Uniform to give Madam to hang on the wall... *And* make Agnes Bradley be Back... Pregnant...

It was when they came to that sudden halt at the door of Madam's Office with its warning sign... Knock Before Entering that Fantasy and Prayer fled from Emma's mind and reality took over. A girl In Disgrace *never* came back ON A VISIT.

THE SHUTTER FALLS

Norman Malcolm Macdonald

THE HERRING TRADE
A hundred years ago

Just pictures now

A man in a lovely gray suit
　　Moves among the fevered workers
A black melodeon under his arm

An elegant Victorian photographer
Come to the herring town
To take likenesses
Of the herring women
Gutting and packing like furies
The full fish

Ceit from the Isle of Lewis
Just one of them
Her first season

　　　I am going to take your picture
　　　Hold very still please

He touches a herring scale on her cheek
One hundred years ago
A glittering sequin
Stuck fast to her skin

He picks off the silver scale
One delicate tug of a fingernail

He has a smell of scent on him

Ceit looks down
Down at the short-bladed gutting knife
The *cutag*
She grips in her right hand
Looks down at the fingers on her left hand
Cupped tenderly around a full herring

Do all you lasses
Leave a curl showing?

Indeed
A piece of our hair
And it lying out on our forehead

The bulky camera is stood up
The photographer behind it

THE SHUTTER FALLS

Muffled in a black shawl
His head in darkness his eyes
Peer through the lens

Each of Ceit's fingers is bound
Bound in a strip of bloody calico
Monumental
She stands in huge leather boots
Her body is wrapped in shapeless oilskin
Tight-bound hair beneath a bright *beannag*
One dark lock let loose on her forehead

The clack of the shutter
Freezes the picture
    The photographer watches her hands
    Dance among the herring
    Ceit's bandaged fingers
    Dance among the herring
    Her naked white arms
    Spattered
    With flecks of pink gut
    The knife in her right hand
    Pulls the entrails from a herring every two seconds
    She flings each gutted fish behind her
    Into the right tub
    Without looking
    With a half-twist of her left wrist

                         THE SHUTTER FALLS

Selection in an instant
By hand
And by eye
The Selections:
Large Fulls
Fulls
Mattie Fulls
Maidens
Only the top gut is removed
The roe and the sperm remain
Full fish prime herring top season
No spent fish
Not yet
Some tornbellies
Naturally

The girls take the tornbellies back to the huts

"The women engaged in this industry
Are worth much consideration
We have been much impressed
With their high standard of conduct
Their reticence
Their dignity"

**View of the Fisher Girls
Lit by the Flares**

The women in line behind the farlane
Cut off at the waist
Before them a mound of dead blue fish
They look into my lens with tired eyes
Her kiss-curl is matted now
The cooper's mouth is open
Crying for more salt
The curer is there
In gold watch and stretched chain
Prices are down in Petersburg

After the exposure
The plate is ripped out of the camera
The first thing the girls
Bought at the herring port
A mirror
A mirror
To hang on the wall of the hut
And a lamp
Then they bought dishes
Fancy crockery from the Baltic

At the end of the season
They will cast lots
For the mirror

The lamp and the dishes
And take home their luck

We stow our best clothes in our cists
Take them out only
On Sundays

The herring is a very symmetrical fish
Its distinguishing features
Are the head
And the belly
There are no eyelids
The eyes are large and extremely beautiful
Strange markings may be seen beneath the delicate
                                                    scales
These are compared by fishermen to a herring net
When the mouth closes well-defined outlines are
                                                    seen

Fishermen say
They resemble a fishing boat
With the mast
In the very position it should be in
When the boat
Is engaged in fishing

I had to find a master first
I would go if he would take me

THE SHUTTER FALLS   **119**

If he gave me a gold piece I was tied to him
The carpenter made me a wooden cist
On board the ship we lay on deck in rows
Like herring unselected
The Enchanted Isles soon hove in sight
Our signal to be sea-sick
The master gave me a gutting-knife
He named me coiler and the first day was a test
The other gear we brought ourselves
A blanket and a counterpane
A curtain for our bed
Yellow calico for our fingers
Oilskins and boots and rubber apron
We left our name in the Stornoway shop
Our name was good
Till we came back home

"Upon rising early one morning
I came upon no less than twenty-four
Of the Lewis gutting women
They stand upon the pier head
Awaiting the fishing boats
They knit for their men as they sing"

I'm fearful for you fresh at sea
That the Saxon man will trick you
I'm fearful for you fresh at sea

THE SHUTTER FALLS

That the wind or sail will take you

"There is something repellent
In the idea of nine women
Having to share one room
To sleep and to eat
To dress and undress
In the very limited space
One is sorry
They have no other place
To receive their friends
To make merry
As they like to on a Saturday evening
By singing psalms
Or by very vigorous dancing"

View of Lewis Gutting Crew
Three Lewis women stand close together
Two gutters and their packer
The hands of the girl in the middle
Are each held in a partner's hand
The woman on the left has her right hand
Upon her own right hip
The woman on the right has her left hand
Tucked into her apron bib
Upon her own left breast

The girl in the centre
Her hands held gently
Has her innocence shielded by experience

In this View
"In my dressing station
I nursed many women
Some had as many as eight
Salt sores to treat
Prayer and Bandages"

I'll not be a herring packer
I'll stand up and gut

Look at her packing there
Reaching down into the bottom of the barrel
Her rump ever up
The cooper behind her with his hoops of cane
Head in and out of the mouth of the barrel
Bandaged hands ladling up herring
Laying them out
Bellies up
One row this way one row that
Up and down

Barrel and tub
Forever bent
A black hen with her bound claws
The cock standing over her

I shall not pack
Bellies up
I will stand up straight
And get the art of the knife

THE GREENGROCER
AND THE HERO

Robin Jenkins

THE HILDERSONS CAME TO Lunderston from South Africa: Mr and Mrs Andrew Hilderson, their daughter Daphne aged 7, and their son Gary aged 3. The children had been born in Johannesburg and had Cockney-sounding accents to prove it, but the parents were Scottish, with only the faintest of outlandish twangs. So far as anyone knew they had had no previous connection with Lunderston. Presumably they chose it because it was a beautiful quiet little backwater where the absence of anything sinister or violent above or below the surface — it was just before the coming of the Americans — must have been a great relief after the strains of a country in which, in a manner of speaking, millions of blacks were kept chained like dogs and one day were sure to break loose and savage their masters. Mr Hilderson was young to be retired from whatever his business had been and yet he seemed to have plenty of money, for he bought Goatfell House, one of the mansions in Ailsa Park, the very select residential area overlooking the town. According to their charwoman, Mrs McLean, they had it

THE GREENGROCER AND THE HERO

adorned with various African objects, some of which she did not approve of, such as wooden statues of black women whose bottoms were much too big. What Mrs McLean also did not like was Mrs Hilderson's habit of coming into the kitchen to have a coffee with her. That was all right, though a bit forward of her really, but what disturbed Mrs McLean was that Mrs Hilderson kept confusing her with a servant she had had in Johannesburg called Hannah. That was all right too, except that Hannah had been coal black. Still, the wages were good, and Mr Hilderson thought nothing of running her home in his big black car, a Daimler, which had all her neighbours in the council housing scheme at their windows, the first time it happened, thinking that somebody had died and this was the undertaker arriving. Lying in bed beside her husband Archie, Mrs McLean once had tried to imagine Mr Hilderson thrashing a negro with a whip. It had been so comically unlikely that she had laughed aloud, to Archie's puzzlement. Mr Hilderson was one of the gentlest men she had ever met: so much so it was more of a fault than a virtue, in that he had no control over his children, especially Gary, who was allowed to do as he pleased.

It would have been an exaggeration and an injustice to call Gary Hilderson a problem child. From the age of 3, when he first arrived in Lunderston, he was a "bloody wee nuisance", to use Mrs McLean's words, echoed by many, but most people, she included, liked

him nonetheless. It was hard to believe that any child could pay no heed to anyone's instructions or pleas, without seeming insolent, but Gary managed it with ease. As Mrs McLean told her grunting Archie, he had charm.

Refusing to be offended himself, whatever was said or done to him, Gary was readily forgiven for any offence he caused. Besides, he was a bright, happy, handsome little boy. Teachers went against their principles and made excuses for him: though one or two more percipient than the others wondered if what was wrong with him was that he did not have any instinctive notion of right and wrong. Other children accused him of stealing their pencils or comics. He would laugh and say that he had just been borrowing them. In vain it was pointed out to him that borrowing without any intention of giving back was the same as stealing. Why should he be a thief though, when he could afford to buy all the pencils and comics he wanted? Discreetly, he was seen by a child psychologist who assured his parents and the school authorities that there was nothing to worry about. Gary had a richer and more complex personality than most children, so it was not surprising that in expressing it he should now and then indulge in unusual activities. One of those however caused anxiety: he hurt people, both physically and mentally, without apparently being aware of it. If it was brought to his notice that holding a magnifying glass to someone's neck on a hot day was a cruel thing to do, he would be at a loss because if it had been done to

him he wouldn't have made a fuss. He would just have waited till he got a chance to do it back.

Mr Hilderson did not mix much in Lunderston society but he joined the golf club and played regularly with three members of retirement age, two ex-bankers and an ex-accountant. Lunderston was a hilly course, particularly the fourth hole. One morning while playing it he was taken ill. Brought home by his playing partners who afterwards resumed their game, for it was a fine May morning, he died three days later in bed. He was only 51.

Lunderston waited to see what the stricken family would do. It was thought that they would go back to South Africa, for Mrs Hilderson was known to grumble about the expense of servants in Scotland and Daphne wasn't happy at the local Academy, where it was an embarrassment to her to find in her classes, sitting side by side with her, black boys and girls, sons and daughters of American service-men from the base. Moreover, she found the air of Lunderston, which the natives called bracing, cold and debilitating. As for Gary, he was enjoying himself at school, though hardly excelling as a scholar. It didn't matter to him whether they went or stayed.

They stayed, or rather Mrs Hilderson and Gary did. Daphne finished her education at Glasgow University and then departed. That she should be willing to leave her mother, and that her mother was prepared to let her go alone, were matters discussed in tea-rooms and at bridge parties, but not too earnestly, for after all the Hildersons were incomers, for whom the

town was not accountable.

Gary was 16 when his sister went away. It was supposed at first that he had refused to go with her because he did not want to leave his mother, but it soon became known that the real reason was Sadie Rankin, daughter of Councillor Rankin, one of the town's greengrocers.

Years later, when he had become famous or infamous, according to your interpretation of the event he took part in, Gary's affair with Sadie was remembered as sad and romantic, like Romeo and Juliet's, but at the time it was generally agreed to be unfortunate, not to say disgraceful.

Sadie then was a few months older than Gary but not any more academically inclined, though sharp-witted. It was said in her defence that she had been led astray by the conscienceless young rogue with the yellow curls, but those who knew her well were doubtful, Sadie had always struck them as not easily persuaded to do what she didn't want to do and what wasn't to her advantage. She was ambitious too, and having seen the inside of Goatfell House probably fancied herself as its mistress one day. In any case, whatever the ins and outs of it were, she became pregnant and Gary was the father.

The scandal involved the school and the kirk, as well as the parents of the culprits, but the whole town was interested. The headmaster impetuously expelled them both: which many considered unjust, in that the crime, if it could be called a crime, had not been

THE GREENGROCER AND THE HERO

committed on his premises. According to Sadie's unabashed confession to her parents fornication had taken place in Goatfell House, on top of a lion's skin, in her own bedroom in her parent's bungalow, and on the bank of the Balgie Burn, near the Episcopal church. When her mother in anguish asked why no precautions had been used Sadie shrugged and shifted the gum from one side of her mouth to the other: giving the impression that she had seen no reason to try and thwart nature's purpose. The Pope would have been pleased but not her parents, though as good presbyterians they could not say so. When they dashed in their car up the hill to Goatfell House to share their trauma with Mrs Hilderson she refused to open the door, though Jack swore he saw her keeking at them from behind a curtain. Reached by telephone, she said curtly that she had been informed (no doubt by her unscrupulous son) that their daughter was promiscuous, so why pick on Gary? When the Rankins had recovered from the shock of that insult they interrogated Sadie again, this time determined to get the truth out of her even if they had to use thumb screws. Coolly she admitted, using words that her parents had not known she knew, that while other boys might have fingered her breasts and private parts Gary was her only penetrator. When the baby was born they would see that it had his yellow hair.

Most of Lunderston believed her, not because they thought her truthful but because they knew her to be sly and resolute, as well as small, dark, passionate,

ambitious, and big-breasted. Whether or not she would make a good mother she certainly had the equipment to entice young men, especially one like Gary Hilderson who didn't give a damn for consequences.

Thanks to the efforts of old Mr Henderson, minister of the church where the Rankins and Mrs Hilderson worshipped (if her rare silent appearances could be so described) a marriage was arranged, Gary having admitted that he probably was the father. Mrs Rankin was pleased, though she pretended that she had consented for the sake of the child. Her husband made no attempt to hide his jubilation. Though his politics were more idiosyncratic than doctrinaire he made such a practice of condemning Communists and Socialists that his friends affectionately called him a wee Fascist. South Africa was one of his favourite countries. Other greengrocers might sell its produce furtively, he did it proudly. He would not, he said, have imprisoned the black leader Mandela, he would have hanged him and all troublemakers like him. So he was delighted at the prospect of having a South African son-in-law, particularly one so handsome and well-to-do.

Gary himself agreed to the marriage without fuss, and wasn't a bit flustered when Sadie's parents came home one evening earlier than expected and found him in bed naked with Sadie who was naked too. "It's all right, Annie," the councillor whispered to his wife, after the confrontation. "They're as good as man and wife."

Sadie demanded and was promised a big wedding in St Cuthbert's. She would be married in white, even if she was known or even seen to be pregnant. It was just old-fashioned stupid superstition that brides had to be virgins. Mr Henderson, belonging to a kirk that moved with the times, acquiesced, but many of his parishioners were outraged.

Two weeks before the wedding Gary vanished. His mother protested that she hadn't known he was going and didn't know where he had gone. The Rankins did not believe her, though she was telling the truth. Then four days after his disappearance she had a telephone call from South Africa. It was Gary asking for money. He said he was too young to get married. He wanted to see the world and have adventures. If she saw Sadie would she convey his apologies?

She did not see Sadie, she took care not to, but she spoke to her and to her parents on the telephone. She was sorry about the child, she said, and offered to contribute towards its keep; but the marriage would have been a disaster, they all ought to be glad that it hadn't taken place, even if the cancellation had come rather late.

The Rankins were not glad. Mrs Rankin had to go to the doctor for pills to stop her palpitations: she was afraid she was going to have a heart attack. Sadie at first was quiet and pale; then one evening while her parents were trying to console her she let out a prolonged scream, like a pig being slaughtered. She

said nothing, just went on screaming, with her hands contorted into claws. Whose face, wondered her father, was she minded to scart? Gary's? But he was thousands of miles away. God's? He was even further. Mine, for singing his praises? Her mother's, for giving her birth? Poor Sadie during those weeks after being cruelly jilted often muttered that she wished she had never been born. They knew that, being young, she would get over it, but they had the sense not to tell her so: better let her find it out for herself.

The councillor's disappointment was as grievous as his daughter's. His hero had behaved worse than a Communist. Gary had let down not only Sadie and Sadie's family but the whole of Western civilisation. If they had known about it in the Kremlin they would have laughed. Recklessly, before witnesses, he vowed that if young Hilderson was ever to set foot in Lunderston again he, Jack Rankin, as God was his witness, would give him the thrashing he deserved. Those who heard about the threat smiled, for Jack though game was only five feet four inches in height and weighed no more than a sackful of lettuce, whereas Hilderson at sixteen was six feet and twelve stones.

The baby was safely born, a yellow-haired, blue-eyed boy, the image of his father. He was christened John after his grandfather, but Sadie insisted that one of his names be Gary, for she still hoped that Hilderson would come back one day and marry her. Mrs Hilderson did not want to see her grandson but her offer to contribute towards his keep was this time

THE GREENGROCER AND THE HERO

scornfully accepted. It meant that wee John was the best-dressed baby in town and was wheeled about in the most sumptuous pram. Sadie proved a devoted and conscientious mother. She did not, as her parents had feared, blame the child for its father's betrayal of her. When wee John was five and she had at last given up hope of ever seeing his father again she married Rab Fairlie, whose family had been farmers in the district for generations. He was considered a good catch, since he was heir to five hundred fertile acres. Having led many a cow to the bull he had a relaxed attitude towards paternity and found no difficulty in accepting the little bastard as his own, and even less in providing him with a half-sister, and then, with all possible speed, with two more half-sisters and a half brother.

In her big house Mrs Hilderson became a recluse. It was noticed by the postman that she received letters now and then from far-off parts of the world, judging from the stamps. It was assumed that these were from Gary, but where he was or what he was doing Lunderston did not know and did not really care, until one day more than ten years after his jilting of Sadie Rankin, now Sadie Fairlie.

The Melanesia affair had been in the newspapers and every night on television before Lunderston realised that it was personally involved. Sensational events in distant places were seldom the occasion for debate or discussion in the town. Lunderstonians preferred to talk about people and matters nearer to home, such as the deaths of acquaintances or in-

creases in the rates. This was not to say that they took no intelligent interest in the world-shaking happenings reported in big black headlines. They read about them, they watched them on television, and gave them two or three minutes' silent cogitation, but they never felt compelled to rush out into the street and argue about them with passers-by. They had not come up the Clyde on bicycles. They knew that next week there would be another world-shaking happening somewhere else, and the week after that still another. Therefore they took them cannily. This particular one was the attempt by a band of mercenaries to kill the President and topple the Marxist government of a small island in the Indian Ocean.

They had flown in a chartered plane from South Africa. That country was denying any responsibility but nobody was believing it. They had come armed with automatic rifles and grenades. Exiles from the island, political enemies of the present government, had financed the venture and had promised large rewards if it succeeded: £100,000 per man was quoted. Unfortunately for the adventurers, the information given them beforehand turned out to be false. They had been assured that as soon as they appeared the people would rise up in rebellion against their oppressors, who had had the arrogance not only to promise to take from the rich and give to the poor but also had carried it out. The poor, it was thought, recognising the immorality of that redistribution, would be eager to get rid of the Communistic clique who had perpetrated it. The poor, however, being not

THE GREENGROCER AND THE HERO

well educated, for the previous government had been content to keep them illiterate, had not understood that the reforms which they thought were improving their lives were really destroying the economy of the island. Therefore, instead of welcoming the would-be liberators, they furiously attacked them. So did the tiny army. There was a battle at the airport. The invaders were besieged in the control tower. After three days they surrendered, having learned that there was no death penalty on the island, this having been abolished by the tyrants. It was admitted, in very small print, by most British newspapers that the Marxists themselves had not seized power but had been democratically voted into it. The so-called liberators therefore were actually terrorists. Nevertheless, to anyone reading between the lines, and Lunderstonians were as good at that as anyone, it was clear that the only fault found with them by the governments of South Africa, the United States, and Great Britain was that they had ineptly failed.

Eventually the names and photographs of the mercenaries were published. One was Gary Hilderson, of South Africa the media said, but Lunderston knew better. Gary had no mother in that country, and no son either.

Jack Rankin was briskly weighing out three pounds of Kerr's Pinks for old Mrs Brotherow when she broke the news to him, in her gruff voice that was heard all over the shop. "I see there's a picture of a freen of yours in this morning's paper, Jack."

"D'you tell me?" said Jack, laughing. "What paper's

that then?"

"The *Herald,* but I expect it's in them a'. Would you like to see it?" She pulled out the *Glasgow Herald* from her shopping bag and finding the right page showed it to him: so that it was with his hands full of Kerr's Pinks that Jack looked and saw, smiling at him with well-remembered impudence, the father of his favourite grandson.

"He's one of them that tried to tak ower from the Communists on that island," said Mrs Brotherow," and made a mess of it. I'll have twa pounds of Brussel sprouts as well. It says they'll get ten years in jile."

White as a cauliflower, Jack said nothing. Just a few days ago, at a meeting of the Business Club, he had let it be known that he was in sympathy with the heroic liberators and very much hoped they succeeded. Now that enthusiasm had had a bucketful of cold disillusionment poured over it.

For the rest of the morning his heart wasn't in the selling of potatoes and sprouts. He had to go into the back shop and, amidst the smell of over-ripe pears, take a couple of paracetamol tablets, to calm the nerves in his stomach. His mind was spinning like a peerie.

When he went home at lunch-time his wife Annie met him at the door with their own copy of the *Herald.* "Have you seen this?"

"Aye."

"Who showed it to you?"

"Mrs Brotherow."

"She would. Well, as you can see he's still laughing at us."

"God knows when that was taken."

"I'll tell you this, Jack Rankin, if they lib him like Rab does his male lambs I'll be mair than pleased."

Rab did it with his teeth. Maybe the blacks on the island would use a knife. But it wasn't likely. They weren't as savage as all that.

Reading what it said under the photographs Jack learned that South Africa had suggested that the adventurers be sent back there to be tried. Well, South African jails being what they were there was a good chance that Hilderson would be forced to jump out of an eight storey window, on to solid concrete below. But did that apply only to blacks? Jack's mind was still spinning.

"And you were singing their praises," jeered Annie, as they ate their lunch. "Heroes of our age, you called them."

"How was I to know he was one of them?"

"I'm worried about Sadie. He's still the one she fancies, you know."

"You're wrong, Annie. She's got over him long ago. It's wee John we should be worried about. Somebody's bound to tell him that that grinning eedjit's his real faither."

"You can see the likeness."

They would all see it.

"Do you think he'll get paid that £100,000?"

"They didn't succeed, did they?"

"But they tried, they did their best. Two of them were killed. Pity he wasn't one of them. If he does get the money wee John should get a share."

"Wouldn't that be acknowledging that Hilderson's got rights over the boy?"

"He's got nae rights but he's got responsibility. What use will the money be to him in jail?"

"He'll not be in jail long. In South Africa they'll not be classed as criminals. They'll get sentenced to five years maybe, to kid the rest of the world. They'll be set free in six months or less. That's how it'll be done, Annie."

She was used to Jack's telling her how it was done, as if he was Prime Minister and not a small-town greengrocer.

"If he *was* your son-in-law, Jack, you'd be proud of him, wouldn't you? Him killing Communists."

"I expect I would. That's the only way to get rid of Reds."

"They weren't got rid of. And an innocent woman was killed."

"That was just propaganda."

"It showed her body on television. It said she had six weans."

"It didn't show who killed her, did it?"

"They were the ones started it."

"In war accidents happen."

"It wasn't war. They were being paid for it. It was

just a job for them, like selling fruit is for you."

He sighed, Annie would never understand. "Are you going to phone Sadie?"

"You know she doesn't see the paper till late at night, after a' her work's done."

It was too much for her, her work. Moreover she was pregnant again. Rab, he reflected bitterly, could do with libbing himself.

"She should have told the boy long ago that Rab isn't his real faither."

Other children had told him. He had come home weeping. Sadie had had to reassure him with lies.

"Well, she'll have to tell him now, after a' this publicity. What about that crazy woman in Goatfell House? She'll no' ken about this. They say she gets no newspaper and hasn't a television."

"To hell with her. It's our Sadie who concerns me. I'm wondering how she'll take it."

Later that night Sadie arrived at their house with an expression on her face that they were all too familiar with. From the age of three she had often looked fiercely revengeful like this. They assumed that it was Hilderson who had provoked her this time, but they were wrong, it was themselves, her loving and caring parents. Before they could offer her a cup of tea she began a screaming tirade. At first they thought it was Hilderson she was blaming for ruining her life, and though she was exaggerating they were ready to sympathise with her. Then it dawned on them that they were the ones being accused. If it

hadn't been for them, she yelled, she would have married Gary and would have had a wonderful exciting life with him in South Africa and other sunny places instead of being buried alive in a wet hole of a farm with a man that thought he was a bull.

If she had shed tears they would have known that it was her emotions speaking, but she remained dry-eyed, and they saw to their horror that she meant it, every single bitter word: it must have been pent up in her for the past ten years.

"For God's sake, Sadie, think of your weans," said her mother, pouring petrol on to the flames.

Trust Annie to say the wrong thing, thought Jack, but what was the right thing?

At last Sadie grew quieter but not any more reasonable. She would go to Gary, she said. Mrs Hilderson would give her the money. She would visit him in prison. She would take photographs of wee John and show them to him. She would tell him that she would wait for him to come out of prison, even if it took ten more years.

You're forgetting the wean in your wame, thought her father, but he did not say it and hoped that Annie wouldn't say it either.

But Annie did, tartly: she had decided it was time to answer back. "They don't let women as far gone as you are, Sadie, on to planes. And I'd be obliged if you'd be more fair to your faither and me. The marriage was all arranged, in case you don't remember. We arranged it, your faither and me, though we

THE GREENGROCER AND THE HERO

baith thought you were too young. It wasn't us that ran away, it wasn't us that left you in the lurch. We've a' had our disappointments. There was a boy in Greenock once — but I won't go into that. His faither was a foreman in Scott Lithgow's."

And there was a girl in Lochgilphead with red hair, thought Jack.

"Life's like that, Sadie," said her mother. "We want to gang doon one road, it sends us doon anither. It happens to us a'. Rab's no' a bad husband, though no' as bright as we would like. His coos having calves every year and his sheep lambs seems to hae given him the idea that his wife should have weans just as often, but you could hae put a stop to that if you'd kept on the pill."

For God's sake, woman, hold your tongue, prayed Jack. Luckily Sadie wasn't listening to her mother. But then who ever listened to anybody?

A few minutes later Sadie left. Her last words were quiet enough but they terrified her parents. "I think I'll go up and see Mrs Hilderson."

She slammed the door behind her.

"Do you think she will?" asked Annie.

"God knows."

"That's no answer, Jack. He knows all right but he never says. I asked you. Will she go and see Mrs Hilderson?"

"How do I know? All right, I don't think she will. She went once before, didn't she, and was left standing on the doorstep."

"This time they've got something to talk about."

They didn't find out until years later whether or not Sadie went that night and talked to Mrs Hilderson.

The one good thing that came out of the crisis was that wee John learned at last who his real father was. He wasn't a bit shattered. On the contrary, he was thrilled. He liked his stepfather and indeed wanted to be a farmer like him when he grew up, but it was a lot more exciting having a father who was like a hero in a film. It was no good other boys jeering that the adventure had failed. A failed adventurer with grenades in his pocket and an automatic rifle over his shoulder was far more interesting as a father that any successful plumber or joiner. When he was older, wee John told them, he was going to call himself by his true name, John Hilderson. He too would go to dangerous places and kill Communists.

Jack Rankin proved to be right in thinking that Hilderson and his confederates would not be kept in prison long. After six months they were all let out. There were pictures of them on television celebrating with champagne. Asked if they were planning any similar missions some of them replied that wherever there was an atheistic Communist dictatorship, that was a place they would like to go to bring freedom to the people. Hilderson however laughed and said,

"Why not, if the money's good?" He was seen and heard saying it in dozens of countries, including the United States. As a result an anti-Communist organisation there invited him to do a lecture tour. There would be a lot of money in it for him, and since he was young, handsome, white, and brave he would be idolised in and out of bed by rich women. It was, a cynical journalist wrote, an enviable assignment, a fitting reward for a hero of the West. In the Scottish press it was reported with pride that on his way to America he intended to visit his mother, who lived in the small seaside town of Lunderston. It said nothing about his visiting his son, because as yet only in Lunderston was it known that he had one.

Lunderston debated as to how he should be greeted. Some said with public plaudits, one or two with rotten eggs, but the majority came to the opinion that no particular notice should be taken of him, let him enjoy his visit to his mother in peace and then depart. After all it wasn't as if he'd been born in the town, and it ought not to be forgotten that he had treated Councillor Jack Rankin's daughter despicably. At a meeting of the District Council one of its crassest members proposed that there should be a civic reception for "a man who, whatever his faults, had struck a blow on behalf of democracy and freedom." He looked to Councillor Rankin for his seconder and was amazed to be given a scowl quite Stalinish in its malevolence. Being from another town he had no interest in what went on in Lunderston and did not

know that Councillor Rankin's grandson was also Hilderson's son. The proposal was not seconded. As someone pointed out since the council had had to close public lavatories as an economy measure it ought not to squander money on entertaining a man who, according to reports in the newspapers, would have at least half a million dollars showered on him in America.

Jack and Annie Rankin hoped that Hilderson would arrive in the town unannounced, spend a day or two with his mother, and then leave as discreetly, but no, there he was, one evening, on Scottish television, being interviewed after the Scottish news, a programme that most of Lunderston watched. The interviewer, a young woman with a gaudy blouse and purple mouth, was evidently charmed by the tall, fair-haired, bronzed adventurer in the tan suit. The questions she put to him were innocuous, except for one, and this he answered with a humility that not everyone thought genuine: such as Mrs Rankin, who cried: "The hypocrite!" Did he not regret that an innocent woman had been killed? "Very much," he replied, but — and here he tossed back his blond curls — that was the pity of war, wasn't it, that innocents got killed. "Though it could be argued," he added, "that anyone content to live under a Communist dictatorship wasn't really innocent." Then, while in socialist living-rooms throughout Scotland went up the anguished cry 'The bastard!' he laughed boyishly and began to talk of the places in America where he was going to speak. One was Hollywood. He men-

THE GREENGROCER AND THE HERO

tioned the names of some actresses he hoped to meet. The verdict in Lunderston, where there were few socialist living-rooms, was that he had done quite well, but then a man who had faced machine-guns was not going to quail before a few questions asked by a dishy young woman in a red, yellow, and black blouse.

Councillor Rankin could not bear to watch. As soon as Hilderson appeared on the screen he rushed to his bedroom, from where he kept shouting: "Is he still on?" His wife kept shouting back, rather impatiently, that he was. The interview lasted no more than three minutes, which was as well, for every second of it was torture to the councillor. At last his wife cried: "It's finished. You can come ben now." He found that the champion of freedom had been replaced by a dour trade unionist defending his members who were on strike, hardly an improvement, for one of Councillor Rankin's strongest beliefs was that all strikes should be banned by law.

Annie knew what would give him most pain, and at once said it: "We've got to admit he's a very good-looking man. I can see why Sadie fancied him. I wouldn't be surprised if he became a film star himself."

"There was a time when you wanted him to be libbed. I hope Sadie didn't see him."

Three weeks ago Sadie had had her seventh child. If she had been watching Hilderson it was probably while giving suck.

"If I was younger I could fancy him myself. Not that I'm all that old. I'm not fifty yet but you treat me as if I was seventy. I read in the Woman's World about couples of over eighty still making love. When was the last time we did?"

He was appalled by her frivolity while serious matters waited to be discussed. "I didn't mark it on the calendar."

"I did. It was January 4th, six months ago. I'd to beg you, God help me. I have to say that I've had more pleasure in sucking a sweetie, and it didn't last half as long."

Casting up in this matter of marital lovemaking was painful and demeaning to him, so he refrained. He could have said it was Annie who had wanted the change to single beds, and it was she, not he, who put cream on her face every night, who wore a flannel night-gown down to her ankles, and who went to bed with steel curlers in her hair.

"I want to talk seriously, Annie."

"Isn't our love-life a serious subject?"

"About wee John and Hilderson. I'm wondering if I should try and arrange a meeting between them. After all, he *is* the boy's father."

"He's never shown any interest."

"This could be the last chance for them to meet. When wee John grows up and learns that we let the chance go by he might not forgive us. You never know, Hilderson might be pleased and grateful, as he

ought to be. What man wouldn't be proud of having a son like wee John? He might even want to take him with him to America. Mind you, I don't think we would allow that."

"I thought I was the romantic one of the family, Jack."

"You're not a man, Annie. You don't understand a man's feelings about having a son."

"I understand that you've always held it against me that we never had one."

"That's nonsense." But it wasn't really.

"You think of wee John as if he was your son, not your grandson. I'm surprised you'd let Hilderson have him."

He was surprised himself: he hadn't thought of it in that way. "For the boy's sake, Annie, should I make the attempt at least?"

"I'm not sure, Jack. It could be a mistake. You'd have to ask Sadie's permission. And Rab's too. He's the boy's legal guardian."

"All right. I'll ask them."

Next morning big Bella, one of his assistants in the shop, a jocular middle-aged spinster, remarked that it was a pity they couldn't have Hilderson on television every night, look how good it was for business. Women who usually bought their greengroceries from rival establishments came in, as if hoping to see

the blond hero behind the counter. Bella had a figure like two sackfuls of potatoes, but Jack was always as chivalrous towards her as if she was as shapely as Raquel Welsh. Now he was tempted to be rude, especially when she whispered with a wink that she had spent all last night lamenting that Hilderson wasn't in bed beside her. Apples, from South Africa, were close-by, rosy-red; but Bella showed not a blush. Women, he thought, would never be the equals of men, as long as they let themselves be deceived by appearances.

He telephoned Sadie. "I feel we owe it to wee John."

She sounded defeated. "I didn't see him on television. How did he look?"

"I didn't see him either."

"Did Mum see him?"

"Yes." Was Annie right? Had he made a mistake?

"What did she think?"

He couldn't lie. "She thought he was as good-looking as ever."

That started Sadie weeping.

"Look, Sadie love, I'm sorry. I shouldn't have bothered you."

"No, Dad, it's all right. Wee John's his son. He should get a chance to see him, if he wants to. Wee John's always asking about him."

"You don't mind then if I go up to Goatfell House and put it to him?"

"No."

"What about Rab? Would he mind?"

"It's got nothing to do with him."

He let that pass.

"If you see him, Dad, give him my love."

Like hell I will, he cried within. Outwardly he said: "I'll be friendly if he is."

She was weeping louder now.

I should take a gun with me, he thought, and shoot the treacherous bastard.

In the evening Jack drove up the hill to Mrs Hilderson's, dressed as if for church or a funeral or a council meeting. The sun sparkled on the Firth. In the mountains of Arran the Warrior slept, after, so local legend had it, conquering all the evil in the world. It was easy to believe it that evening of blue skies, with roses blooming in every garden and birds singing blithely.

He had heard that Mrs Hilderson had allowed her property to run down, not because she lacked the means to keep it in good order, but because she had lost heart. The big iron gates were rusty, the driveway full of pot-holes and weeds, the rhododendrons overgrown, and the big house itself, with all its blinds down, dismal looking, even in the bright sunshine. Jack might have thought that there was no one living there if it hadn't been for a car at the front door, a red Vauxhall Cavalier. He saw from a sticker that it

belonged to a Glasgow firm of car-hirers. It must be Hilderson's.

Why was it, just when he needed all the power of forgiveness that he was capable of, that he found himself shaking with rage as he thought of the man who had so callously wronged his daughter? For God's sake, Jack, he told himself, you've come to make peace with Hilderson and offer God's greatest gift, a son, not a puling infant either but a splendid little lad of eleven. Even if he rejects your offer, though it's inconceivable that he will, it's up to you, as a man who believes in God, to act calmly and without bitterness. You will simply tell him sorrowfully and with dignity that the loss is his, though he might not realise it until he was old and it was too late. "Don't lose your temper, Jack," Annie had said. She should have known that he never lost his temper. Sometimes he might be more passionate than the occasion called for, but that was because he cared so much for truth and justice. Speaking to Hilderson, and also to Mrs Hilderson if she deigned to show her face, he would subdue his passion and speak humbly, whatever provocations were heaped on him.

With a hand smelling of apples he banged the big knocker in the shape of a lion's head. It should have been shining brass but was green with verdigris.

As he waited he looked down on Lunderston, his native town, which as a councillor it was his duty to look after and protect. Its public lavatories, open now because it was summer, would not be closed again this winter, as they had been last winter: he would

THE GREENGROCER AND THE HERO

see to that. Yonder were those in the West Bay, being well patronised as he could see. Yonder those on Kirk Brae. Yonder those in the gardens behind the supermarket. Only one who loved the town and knew it well could have picked them out. Yonder too was Brisbane Avenue, with its rows of red-roofed bungalows: his was one of those facing the football field. Annie would be sitting in it now, reading the Barbara Cartland romance she had bought that afternoon. Or maybe she would be on the telephone to Sadie, talking about his mission to Hilderson. She had promised to say nothing until he returned with his report, but she was impatient, like most women. In his experience as a councillor and greengrocer it was women who were always complaining, about holes in the pavements or potatoes with rotten insides, and they weren't willing to wait for a decent interval to let things be remedied. They wanted miracles of quickness. Men knew the difficulties and made allowances.

The door opened at last and he was looking at the only man he had ever hated. Though coarser than he had been at sixteen Hilderson was still damnably handsome and carefree.

He was wearing tan slacks, red shirt, cashmere pullover, and dark-eyed shoes, all of the very best quality. His hair was bleached by the sun. It ought by rights to have been cropped like a convict's and he ought to have been wearing prison clothes.

With a great effort Jack smiled. Hilderson was already smiling, with self-satisfaction. He hadn't rec-

ognised Jack as Sadie's father.

"Are you from the local *Herald* ?" he asked.

"The local paper is the Gazette. I am not a reporter. My name is Councillor Rankin."

"Well, if you've come to invite me to a civic do it's not on. I'm flying off to the States tomorrow."

"Tomorrow?"

"To London first and then New York."

"I see. I am not here on behalf of the council, Mr Hilderson. My business is personal and private. Could we step inside?"

"Better not. The house is a bit musty. My mother doesn't keep it aired." Hilderson was grinning, as if he had just seen the joke, whatever it was. "Did you say your name's Rankin?"

"I did."

"Are you a greengrocer?"

"I am."

"Susie's dad?"

"My daughter's name is Sadie."

"Sure, Sadie. How is she? I've heard she's done well for herself, married a farmer and has a dozen kids."

"She has seven. One of them is yours."

"Come off it, councillor. You're not going to pin that on me."

As if it was a bloody medal, thought Jack. He heard and saw seagulls. He imagined they were vultures,

ready to devour a corpse. It was as well he hadn't brought a gun.

"If you recall, Mr Hilderson, you left Lunderston suddenly about eleven years ago because you had got my daughter pregnant."

"Councillor, if I'd pleaded guilty to all the times I've been accused of that I'd be the father of a tribe, not all of them the same colour."

"The marriage was arranged. You sneaked off. It was not the act of an honourable man."

"I was only a boy, councillor, and wasn't there some doubt as to who the father was?"

More than ever the gulls sounded like vultures. "That is an insulting observation, Mr Hilderson. There was no doubt. Your own mother accepted your responsibility. She has been contributing towards the child's upkeep."

"My mother's a bit peculiar."

"The boy happens to be your image."

"When people are looking for resemblances they can always see them. They see them in dogs even."

Jack might have struck him then, though it would have been difficult, Hilderson being much taller and standing on a step, but they were joined by Mrs Hilderson walking with the help of a stick. Jack was amazed to see that her hair was snow white, though she was hardly any older than himself. She did look peculiar. Judging from the faraway look in her eyes she was away with the fairies, as they said in Lunderston. She didn't smell fresh either.

THE GREENGROCER AND THE HERO 155

"What is it, Gary?" she asked. "Who is this person?"

"I'm Councillor Rankin," said that person. "Sadie's father. I've come to ask your son if he would like to meet his son, towards whose keep you have been contributing for the past eleven years. It may be his sense of humour or it could be that his recent experiences have deranged him, but he has denied paternity."

"Does it matter," she asked contemptuously," who your father is?"

She did not wait for an answer, but if she had waited an hour or all night or all year Jack, flabbergasted, could not have given her one. Did it really matter? Whether your father was the murderer hanged for his crime or the judge who had sentenced him you were yourself, you couldn't be blamed for anything you hadn't done yourself. Men who had run the concentration camps during the War had sons and daughters who in Germany today were respectable citizens.

These thoughts were whirling in Jack's mind as Hilderson, laughing, stepped inside and shut the door. Gazing at the green lion Jack wondered where he was. Then he turned to look down at the town below. He felt strange. Were those the spires of Lunderston or of heaven? Annie would scold him for having made a mess of his mission, Sadie would weep, and wee John would be sorely disappointed. Nevertheless he felt that he had succeeded in a way that he could never explain to anyone. He had been let into a secret.

No one would notice any difference in him. Annie would criticise and Bella make fun. He would still be called a wee Fascist. At council meetings his proposals would still be rejected as being far-fetched and impracticable. Behind his back people would still laugh at him, the diminutive greengrocer with the big ideas. All that was true, but he would find it easier to forgive them, because he knew now that they were all, every single one of them, including Communists and shoplifters, special and unique.

It probably would not last, this inspiration, old habits of thought and prejudices would blot it out, but echoes would be with him for the rest of his life.

THE CUTTING-OFF PIECE

(A Dream Play in One Act)

Donald Campbell

*HE SCENE IS A DESERTED building in Glasgow, circa 1900. There is a brazier and a couple of benches. As house lights dim, there is an explosion of thunder, flash of lightning and the sound of falling rain.*

Enter Johnnie Mackay, a young man in his twenties, raggedly dressed, with a cap and neckerchief. Soaked, limping and breathless from running, he sits down by the brazier and takes off his right shoe. Examining the sole, he finds he can put his finger right through it and shakes his head miserably. He lays the shoe aside and pulls off his sock.

Johnnie— 'Glasgow!' *Groans.* 'Lord, what a place!' *He wrings the wetness from his sock and puts both it and the shoe back on.* 'What am I doing here?' *He stands up and takes his jacket off, setting it on the bench to dry. Using his neckerchief as a towel, he wipes the rain from his face.* 'What in the world possessed me to leave

THE CUTTING-OFF PIECE

the North for a place like this?' *Sits again.*
'The green place, they call it in Gaelic — but
I've seen nothing green about it!' *He shrugs.*
'Unless I look in a mirror, for I was green
myself for ever thinking there was a future
in leaving home!' *Thoughtfully, he contemplates a verse:*

'Auld Caithness may look bare and cauld,
When wintry win's blow loud and bauld,
But kind and warm her hearts unfauld....'

He breaks off despairingly. 'Oh, no, no! I'd
give all the money there is in this city — if
it was mine — for one sight of the green
fields of Caithness! Oh, Caithness, Caithness! Why did I ever leave ye for this filthy,
ungenerous hole?'

*Another clap of thunder and lightning. The lights
flicker and go out momentarily. When they come
up again, Jenny Horne, the Caithness Witch, is
discovered centrestage. She shakes out her shawl
and smiles at Johnnie.*

Jenny H— 'Johnnie Mackay, is it no?'

Johnnie— 'Eh?'

Jenny H— 'Johnnie Mackay. Is that no what they call
ye, boy?'

Johnnie— 'That's my name all right.'

Jenny H— 'From Dalmachair?'

Johnnie— 'Thereabouts. But...' *surprised and suspicious,*

'How did ye know?'

Jenny Horne nods in satisfactions, haps her shawl and joins him by the fire,

Jenny H— 'Aye, aye, Johnnie Mackay! It's a bonnie-looking ticket ye are and all, eh?' *As he rises, bristling.* 'Oh, sit ye doun, laddie! Sit ye doun! Dinna be wasting the fire! The Lord knows there's little enough of it!'

They sit down together. Johnnie is puzzled but interested as Jenny Horne relaxes at the fire, loosening her shawl and warming her hands.

'My, my, though! Is this no terrible weather we've been having? It's fair bleetering doun outby!'

Johnnie— 'Well, I know that, wifie!'

She gives him an enquiring glance, which he answers irritably.

Johnnie— 'I was caught in the rain — I got soaked!'

Jenny H— 'Oh Aye, Johnnie! so ye were!'

Johnnie— 'I know all about the weather, wifie! It's ye I'm no sure of! Am I supposed to know you or something?'

Jenny H— 'What makes you think that, Johnnie?'

Johnnie— 'Well, ye seem to know me all right. At least ye have my name!'

Jenny H— 'Your name, eh?' *Sarcastically.* 'And is that all there is intil ye? Your name?'

THE CUTTING-OFF PIECE

Johnnie—	'Now look here, wifie...'
Jenny H—	'And I suppose, if I were to tell ye my name, ye'd know all about me?'
Johnnie—	'It would help, anyway!' *Impatiently.* 'Who are ye? What's your name?' *Eagerly,* 'Are you from Caithness by any chance?' *Jenny Horne laughs out loud.*
Johnnie—	'What's the matter?'
Jenny H—	'Am I from Caithness by any chance?' *She scoffs at him, but her sarcasm is kindly:* 'My word, Johnnie Mackay, it was sharp of ye to spot that — sharp of ye indeed!' *Pauses, eyes him with amusement.* 'Jenny Horne.' *Johnnie can hardly believe his ears.*
Johnnie—	'What? What was that?'
Jennie H—	'Ye asked me my name and I tellt ye!' *Beams.* 'I'm Jenny Horne!' *Johnnie rises slowly, apprehensively, begins to move away. Jenny Horne chuckles at this.*
Johnnie—	'Oh my Lord...'
Jenny H—	'Know me now, do ye?'
Johnnie—	'I know of ye all right! I've heard tell of ye!' *Accusingly,* 'Ye're a witch, that's what ye are! A witch! And I'm taking nothing to do with ye...' *Johnnie tries to leave hurriedly. Without turning, Jenny Horne barks a command which freezes him in his tracks.*
Jenny H—	'Johnnie Mackay! Bide where ye are boy!'

Smiles in satisfaction as she sees he cannot move. 'What d'ye want out there for, anyway? Ye'll only get yourself soaked to the skin all over again! Besides, I'd only have to follow ye!' *Snaps her fingers and beckons him back.* 'Come ye over here and dinna be stupid! I'll no hurt ye!'

Released, Johnnie moves back to his seat, full of fear and wonder.

Johnnie — 'What d'ye want with me, Jenny Horne?'

Jenny H — 'Oh, nothing much!' *Smiles.* 'How long since ye left home, Johnnie?'

Johnnie — 'Four months.' *Shrugs,* 'Four months — and a bittie more.'

Jenny H — 'Why d'ye do it? Why d'ye leave the North?' *Irritably, as he hesitates,* 'Well? Speak up, boy!'

Johnnie — 'Why does anybody leave the North?' *Sheepish,* 'I came to Glasgow to seek my fortune.'

Jenny H — 'I see.' *Sniffs and inspects him,* 'And how're ye getting on?'

Johnnie — 'What?'

Jenny H — 'How much of your fortune have ye made so far?' *Laughs as he turns away angrily from her sarcasm,* 'Ye're no doing all that great, are ye, boy?'

Johnnie — 'I've no money, nowhere to live, no friends. I canna find work, no matter how hard I try!

THE CUTTING-OFF PIECE

I was thrown out of my room a week ago, and my landlady's taken all my belongings against the rent that I owe her. I've no eaten for days and the Lord only knows where I'm going to sleep the night!' *Turns to her,* 'And to cap it all, Mistress Horne, I've a hole in my shoe — so I get my feet wet every time I go out in the rain!'

Jenny H— 'No, ye've no, boy.' *As Johnnie looks puzzled,* 'I've fixed your shoe.'
Amazed, Johnnie slowly lifts his foot and inspects the sole.

Johnnie— 'Well, I'll be...' *Amazed* '...so ye have! How did ye...'

Jenny H— 'Och, say no more, Johnnie!' *Shrugs dismissively,* 'It was nothing, shoes are easily mended. Silly boygies are far more difficult!' *Rises and moves centrestage,* 'What would ye like most in the whole world?' *Cautioning,* 'I'm no saying I can give it til ye, mind!'

Johnnie— 'What would I like?' *Smiles,* 'That's easy — I'd like fine to go home.'

Jenny H— 'Home? Dalmachair, ye mean?'

Johnnie— 'Aye! Dalmachair!'

Jenny H— 'And what would ye do in Dalmachair, Johnnie? Herd the kye again, is it?'

Johnnie— 'It'd be a lot more than I'm doing here! Besides, I'd sooner herd the kye in Dalmachair than be Lord Provost of this city itself!'

Jenny H— 'Would ye now?'

Johnnie— 'Aye, I would that!'

Jenny H— 'Ye're fooling yourself, laddie.' *Smiles and shakes her head,* 'Ye're thinking of the good old days, the best days, the brave and bonnie days of your childhood, when the summer never ended and ye hadna a care in the whole wide world...Oh, I know, Johnnie! I know. It all comes back to ye when the world seems at its darkest. It's at times like that when ye'll maybe hear a voice, a lassie's voice ...' *Raises her arm and gently snaps her fingers* '....singing a sang for ye...'

Lighting change as a young girl is heard singing off stage.

Maggie— So fair-ye-weel, sweet Pulteney Banks,
Where oft-times I've been cheerie,
And fare-ye-weel to the Old Man o Wick
For its there I lost my dearie.
But he's awa, let him be gone,
No longer shall he grieve me;
For I am young and I'm a maid
And another shall receive me.

Enter Maggie Fraser singing. She is a pretty young woman, prettily dressed, thoughtful and demure, pulling petals from a flower she has in her hand. Johnnie is amazed to see her.

Johnnie—	'Maggie! Maggie Fraser!' *Goes to her quickly,* 'Is that yourself, Maggie? Can it really be ye?'
	She turns to him briefly, smiles absently,
Maggie—	'Oh! Oh, hello, Johnnie!'
	She turns away from him again. Feeling helpless, he turns to Jenny Horne for advice. Jenny Horne gestures that he should continue.
Johnnie—	'Well, then, Maggie...' *Awkward,* '..How've ye been keeping?'
Maggie—	'No so bad.' *Smiles.* 'Yourself?'
Johnnie—	'Och...' *Shrugs,* '...I'm fine! Just fine!'
Maggie—	'That's grand, then.'
	Disconcerted by Maggie's apparent lack of interest, Johnnie turns once more to Jenny Horne, who makes insistent signals for him to continue.
Johnnie—	'I've ..eh..I've fair been missing ye, Maggie!' *This interests Maggie, who turns back to face him directly for the first time:*
Maggie—	'Missing me? D'ye tell me that, now?'
Johnnie—	'Oh, Aye, Maggie! I have and all!'
	She moves closer to him,
Maggie—	'And how would ye be doing that, Johnnie?'
Johnnie—	'Och, Maggie! Ye know yourself!'
	Her voice is soft and seductive, exciting him as she moves even closer,
Maggie—	'I'd have thought ye'd forgotten all about me long since.'

THE CUTTING-OFF PIECE   **167**

Johnnie— 'Oh! Maggie! How could I ever do that?'
He reaches to embrace her. She flounces away, laughing.

Maggie— 'Oh! Johnnie Mackay! Ye're a terrible man, so ye are!' *Harder*, 'Ye're making fun of me, I think.'

Johnnie— 'No!'

Maggie— 'So ye've been missing me, have ye?'

Johnnie— 'More than ye can ever know!'

Maggie— 'I dinna believe ye!'

Johnnie— 'Maggie...'

Maggie— 'Well why should I! Ye've been off til Glasgow for months...'

Johnnie— 'Ach, Glasgow!'

Maggie— '...and they do say that the Glasgow lassies are fine and bonny...'

Johnnie— 'That's nonsense!'

Maggie— 'What?'

Johnnie— 'Nonsense, I'm telling ye!' *Scoffs*, 'Glasgow lassies bonnie? Where did ye ever hear the like of that?'

Maggie— 'Well...are they no?'

Johnnie— 'Not a bit of it! Oh, they're great swells, I'll grant ye — with their fine clothes and all their airs and graces! If ye call that bonnie, they're bonnie enough! But I'll tell ye this, Maggie — I never met a Glasgow lassie yet that could as much as hold a candle to the plainest lassickie ye'd meet on any Caithness farm!'

THE CUTTING-OFF PIECE

Maggie —	'Now, Johnnie...'
Johnnie —	'It's true, I'm telling ye! The Glasgow lassies, they're just awful! Yellow as Chinamen, most of them!'
Maggie —	'Chinamen?'
Johnnie —	'Aye, ye needna laugh! I'll tell ye this and all — I've yet to meet a lassie in Glasgow that's got as much as a single tooth in her head that she can call her own!'
Maggie —	'Surely never!'
Johnnie —	'Rotten! Just like everything else in that city. Rotten to the very core!'
	He turns away from her in his anger
Maggie —	'Glasgow's no what it's cracked up to be, then?'
Johnnie —	'No!'
Maggie —	'At least, no as far as lassies are concerned?'
	He turns back to her emotionally
Johnnie —	'Maggie, even if it was, d'ye think I'd ever find a woman — in Glasgow or anywhere else in the whole wide world! — that'd make me forget about ye?'
	She turns away from him with a capricious sniff. He approaches her very seriously,
Johnnie —	'Why d'ye do it, Maggie?'
Maggie —	'Do what?'
Johnnie —	'Ye know what I'm talking about!'
	Angrily, he seizes her and forces her to face him. She squeals in surprise,

THE CUTTING-OFF PIECE   169

Maggie —	'Johnnie!'
Johnnie —	'Why d'ye throw me over for that thick-headed dunce, Muirhead?'
Maggie —	'Throw ye over?'
Johnnie —	'Why d'ye leave me to go off with him? Ye know fine that I can do far more for ye than he ever could!'
Maggie —	'Oh, could ye now?'
Johnnie —	'A hundred times more!' *Lets her go wearily,* 'Ye cut me to the very heart when ye left!'
Maggie —	'My word!' *With cold sarcasm,* 'It seems to me, Johnnie Mackay, that your memory's serving ye poorly!' *Angrily,* 'It's no me that's left, boy! I'm still here!' *Accusingly,* 'It was ye that left me to go running off to Glasgow....'
Johnnie —	'But it was for ye that I did it, Maggie! Ye know that yourself!'
Maggie —	'What?'
Johnnie —	'D'ye think I'd ever have dreamt of leaving home if ye hadna thrown me over for Jock Muirhead?'
Maggie —	'Ye mean...' *Incredulous, begins to laugh,* 'ye went off til Glasgow because of me and Jock....Lord bless me, now I've heard every-thing!'
Johnnie —	'What's so funny?'
Maggie —	'I never heard the like in all my born days!' *Stops laughing and gives him a withering look.*

THE CUTTING-OFF PIECE

'And where did ye think that was going to get ye?'

Johnnie — 'I thought — I still think — that, if I canna have ye, then I'd be as well making an effort at improving myself, getting on a bit in the world...'

Maggie — 'Make your fortune?'

Johnnie — 'Make something anyway?' *Rejects her derision with intensity.* 'Do something! Be something!' *Shrugs.* 'Then, maybe later on, I could come home....'

Maggie — 'And there I'd be, pining away for ye?' *Scoffs.* 'My word, boy, ye've a good conceit of yourself, have you no?'

Johnnie — 'If ye cared for me at all, ye'd wait.'

Maggie — 'Wait for what? And for how long? What kind of fool d'ye take me for?'

Johnnie — 'It wadna be so bad, Maggie! I'd be home as often as I could — and we could always write...'

Maggie — 'Write? Oh Aye, Johnnie! It's ye that's the great chiel for the writing, is it no?' *Contemptuously.* 'I've had your letters — and your poems!'

Johnnie — 'What's the matter with my poems?'

Maggie — 'They're full of words, that's what's the matter with them! Nothing but words — that's all ye are, Johnnie Mackay! Nothing but talk, empty talk!' *Turns on him, hands on hips, meaning business.* 'I'll tell ye this

much, Johnnie Mackay — I never cared two
hoots for Jock Muirhead afore ye left! If ye'd
wanted me then — really wanted me, instead of talking about it all the time — ye
could have had me for the snap of your
fingers! But ye, ye never had the spunk to
do anything but dream and write your
stupid poetry! Poor Jock's maybe no so
bonnie-looking — and it's certain he's no
much of a hand for poetry — but he's
enough of a man to know how to give a
lassie what she wants! So I'm going to marry
Jock Muirhead....'

Johnnie— 'Marry him?'

Maggie— 'Ye heard me! I'll marry Jock just as soon as
he'll have me — and ye can go til the very
devil!'

She starts to storm out. Johnnie grabs her arm.

Johnnie— 'Maggie, dinna! Whatever ye do, dinna
leave...'

Maggie— 'Leave me alone, ye fool!' *Breaks his grip.*
'It's a man I'm after, Johnnie Mackay. No
a...a blooming dictionary!'

*Exit Maggie. Johnnie trys to follow but he finds
he cannot.*

Johnnie— 'Maggie, come back! Please come back!
Dinna leave me like this! Dinna go off and
leave me here like this!'

*Lighting change. Jenny Horne moves centrestage
once more.*

Jenny H—	'Let her go, Johnnie! Let her go!' *As Johnnie turns to her in stunned confusion.* 'She's gone, boy. Ye canna follow her!' *She goes to the brazier and warms her hands.*
Johnnie—	'No.' *Coming to himself.* 'She was never really there anyway, was she? It was only a...' *Sighs* '...only a fancy?'
Jenny H—	'There are all kinds of fancies, Johnnie.'
Johnnie—	'How d'ye mean?'
Jenny H—	'Was Maggie ever real? Was she no always a fancy?'
Johnnie—	'No! I knew her. I loved her. I still love her!'
Jenny H—	'Are ye sure of that, boy?'
Johnnie—	'Of course I'm sure! Listen, Mistress Horne, I don't know what's going on here, I don't know what kind of...mystery ye're weaving or what kind of game ye're playing with me, but I do know this! Maggie Fraser is real! She works at Dalmachair House and I was courting her until...'
Jenny H—	'Oh, I'll no gainsay that, boy! But is that the Maggie ye love, eh? Is the Maggie ye knew in Dalmachair the same lassie that was here even now?'
Johnnie—	'Aye... I think so.' *Grows uncertain.* 'I spoke to her, touched her. She was just the same as always, only...'
Jenny H—	'Aye?'
Johnnie—	'Well, I never knew her to be so...cruel afore this. I mean, the things she said about my

poetry!' *Grows defensive as Jenny Horne turns away with a chuckle.* 'She used to love my poetry — everybody did!'

Jenny H— 'Did they now?'

Johnnie— 'They did and all, so! Even my own worst enemy — Jock Muirhead himself — had til gie in that I could turn a bonnie verse when the mood was on me.' *Smiles in reminiscence.* 'I mind once, I made a rhyme about the lads of Waster. They used to roar it out in the bothies when the drink was in!'

To Johnnie's surprise and delight, Jenny Horne quotes the verse.

Jenny H— 'O' a' the happy lads I know'
'Mang burly Caithness ploomen,
To beat the Waster lads I trow,
Ye'll fin' there are but few, man!
Straicht is the furrow they can draw,
Their mind's as prood's their Master's,
They winna wi' a slave whip ca',
The merry lads o' Waster!

Johnnie— 'Ye know it!'

Jenny Horne shrugs and moves upstage,

Jenny H— 'Ye'd be surprised at all that I know, Johnnie — especially when it comes to the merry lads of Waster!'

Lighting change as Jenny Horne raises her arm and snaps her fingers.

Davie (off)—'It'll never work, Neil! Ye'll get the both of us into trouble!'

Neil *(off)* — 'Ach, dinna be foolish, man! I know what I'm doing!'

Enter Neil Gow and Dave Cormack, two country lads. Neil has a bottle in his hand. Neither of them notice Johnnie, who grins with delight as he sees them.

Davie — 'But she's bound to find us out, Neil. Sooner or later....'

Neil — 'Good Lord, boy — of course she will! And I'll no be long in making it up to her when she does. It's only a joke — I'm no after thieving from the woman!'

Davie — 'She'll never fall for it, Neil — never in a hundred years.' *With a gloomy shake of the head,* 'She'll see right through us!'

Neil — 'Oh, for the love of...' *with impatience,* 'Davie Cormack, what's the matter with ye, man? Where's your sense of adventure? Listen, we're needing a bottle for tonight, are we no?'

Davie — 'Aye — but how can we no just walk in and buy it like always? We've got the money.'

Neil — 'Of course we've got the money!' *Groans.* 'There's no problem about the money. It's just that it's more fun this way. Just trust me, Davie, eh? Do what I tell ye and trust me.'

Davie sees Johnnie, grins and pulls at Neil's sleeve.

Davie — 'Neil! Look who's here!'

THE CUTTING-OFF PIECE   175

Neil turns and sees Johnnie, who nods to them both.

Johnnie — 'It's yourself, Neil. Davie.'

Neil — 'Well, I'll be... Johnnie Mackay! How're ye doing, boy? How're ye doing?'

Both men make much of Johnnie.

Davie — 'It's great to see ye, man!'

Neil — 'Where did ye spring from? We thought ye were in Glasgow?'

Johnnie — 'Well, ye see...' Looks to Jenny Horne, who shrugs and turns her back on them all '...it's a long story.'

Neil — 'Well, never heed even now! Ye're home again, that's the main thing.'

Davie — 'Just in time and all! Eh, Neil?'

Johnnie — 'How's that?'

Neil — 'By Jove, Davie — ye're right enough!' To Johnnie, 'It's the Cutting-off Piece the night, boy!'

Johnnie — 'The Cutting-off Piece!'

Neil — 'Aye, it's come round again! And we'll be looking til ye for a poem or two or maybe a song!' Slaps Johnnie on the shoulder. 'My, my, boy — but we've fair been missing ye about the place! Is that no right, Davie?'

Davie — 'Aye, Neil.' To Johnnie. 'We've no seen ye since the nicht ye gave Jock Muirhead his licks on the Dalmachair brig!'

Neil — 'Oooh, Aye! Thon was a grand fecht that, eh?'

THE CUTTING-OFF PIECE

Johnnie —	'That was the nicht afore I left for Glasgow.' *Sadly, to himself,* 'I'd forgotten all about it!' *Brighter:* 'And how is Muirhead, eh? Still throwing his weight about as usual?' *Neil and Davie are suddenly very serious.*
Neil —	'Oh, Johnnie! Thon's a sad case, a very sad case, indeed!'
Davie —	'An awful business!'
Johnnie —	'What's the matter?'
Davie —	'Did ye no hear?'
Johnnie —	'Hear what?'
Neil —	'Well, Johnnie, as ye know yourself, I cared for Jock. He was always...ach, I don't know, the man never seemed to have any humour in him! I reckon it was the kirk that did it, eh Davie?'
Davie —	'Could be!'
Neil —	'A fine strapping lad like Jock!' *Shakes his head regretfully.* 'I was right sorry to see him go!'
Johnnie —	'What d'ye mean, Neil?' *Horrified.* 'Ye're no telling me that...Jock's no...he's no dead, is he?' *Neil and Davie exchange surprised looks, then burst out laughing.*
Neil —	'Dead? Hits, no, man! It's worse than that!'
Davie —	'He's married, Johnnie! Jock Muirhead's a married man!'
Neil —	'Married, married, married! Who'd ever

	have thought it?'
Johnnie —	'Married? Who'd he marry?'
Neil —	'Eh?'
Johnnie —	'Who's Jock married? Who's the lassie?'
Davie —	'Maggie Fraser, Johnnie? Who else?'
Johnnie —	'Oh, no!'
Neil —	'Aye, and that's another thing and all! Maggie Fraser!'
Davie —	'The Flower of Dalmachair!'
Neil —	'That's what we called her! She had all the menfolk up til ninety! Ye had a notion of her yourself, Johnnie, as I mind?'
Johnnie —	'Aye. I had that.'
Davie —	'Well, ye've had a lucky escape, boy! right, Neil?'
Neil —	'Ye have the rights of it there, Davie — for a more sour-faced, ill-natured, mean-hearted limmer of woman I've never met in my life! It's been barely a month since she captured Muirhead and she's been the ruin of him already. Running him ragged, so she is!'
Johnnie —	'I canna believe it! No Maggie!'
Neil —	'Aye, Maggie! Ye know what they say, boy — we're all born but we're no all buried and we never know what's in front of us! As Davie says, ye've had a lucky escape — be thankful ye're living single!' *Slaps Johnnie on the shoulder and changes the subject.* 'Anyway, let's forget all about Muirhead's miser-

able marriage and turn our minds til happier matters! Johnnie, Davie and I are about to transact a wee transaction,' *taps his nose slyly,* 'with Mistress Kate Angus!'

Davie — 'Oh, Neil! Can we forget about that now?'

Neil — 'Of course we canna! Johnnie, did ye ever see the like of this man here?' *Contemptuously*: 'Feared of a little bit of pleasure and excitement!'

Johnnie — 'Is this a ploy ye've got on, Neil?'

Davie — 'Some ploy!'

Neil — 'Oh, never heed him, Johnnie!' *Holds up the bottle.* 'What's this I have in my hand?'

Puzzled but amused, Johnnie shrugs.

Johnnie — 'Looks like a bottle of whisky.'

Neil turns triumphantly to the sceptical Davie:

Neil — 'Ye see?'

Davie — 'Looks like!'

Johnnie — 'What's the matter?'

Davie — 'The bottle's empty, Johnnie! At least, it was — afore Neil filled it with water from the burn!'

Neil — 'Johnnie, I'm about to turn water intil whisky!' *Grins.* 'Whisky, mind — no wine! I'm no that ambitious!' *Hands the bottle to Davie.* 'Dinna forget what I tellt ye — and we'll see what happens! Watch this, Johnnie!' *Moves upstage and calls off,* 'Mistress Angus! Mistress Angus! Could ye come down here a minute? It's Neil Gow — I'd like a word with

THE CUTTING-OFF PIECE

ye!'

He turns to the others and winks. Enter Jenny Smith, a bright young bar-maid.

Jenny S— 'Hello, Neil! What're ye after?'

Neil— 'Jenny, it's yourself! Is your mistress in?'

Jenny S— 'She's at her books.' *Looks over to the others:* 'Hello there, Davie!' *Sees Johnnie and does a double-take.* 'Johnnie Mackay? Is that ye, boy?' *Goes to him.* 'Home from Glasgow, is it?'

Neil— 'Aye, he's home from Glasgow! He'll be at the Cutting-off Piece the night if ye want him! Listen, Jenny, if Mistress Angus is at her books, I'd no like to disturb her, but...' *Impatiently, as he realises that Jenny is too taken up with Johnnie to listen to him,* 'Are ye listening to me, lassie?'

Jenny S— 'Aye. What is it?'

Neil— 'The thing is, Jenny, I find myself in need of a bottle of Old Pulteney — for the Cutting-off Piece, ye know — and I was wondering if....'

Jenny S— 'We're closed, Neil.'

Neil— 'Closed? Oh, Jenny — come on! Surely ye can oblige a regular customer?' *Coaxes,* 'Eh, Jenny?' *As she considers it,* 'Surely ye'll no let me down?'

Jenny S— 'Oh, all right! Just wait there even now!' *Leaving, she gives Johnnie a big smile.* 'Great to see ye home, Johnnie!'

Exit Jenny S. Neil rubs his hands in delighted anticipation:

Neil — 'Oooh, it's going like a clock!' *Nudges Johnnie,* 'Ye watch your work, boy, and ye'll be all right there the night!'

Jenny S. comes back with a bottle of whisky.

Jenny S — 'Here ye are, Neil. Just this once, mind!'

Neil — 'That's grand, Jenny! That's clinking!' *Takes the bottle.* 'Ye're a good lassie!'

Jenny S — 'That'll be two shillings, Neil.'

Neil — 'What?'

Jenny S — 'The price of the whisky.'

Neil — 'Oh, of course!' *Digs in his pockets.* 'Here, is that no just like the thing, eh? I've come out without my money! Davie, have ye a couple...' *as Davie shakes his head,* '...what about yourself, Johnnie?..' *as Johnnie does likewise,* 'ah well, then! Jenny, I don't suppose Mistress Angus would mind if...'

Jenny S — 'Two shillings, Neil!'

Neil — 'Surely she'd let me hand the money in later on?'

Jenny S — 'Oh, I doubt that!'

Neil — 'Well, ye could always ask her, lassie!' *Softer, coaxing again,* 'It's worth a try, Jenny, eh? Otherwise, I'll have to go all the way back..'

Jenny S — 'Oh, all right! Just bide where ye are until I come back.'

THE CUTTING-OFF PIECE

Neil —   'Right ye are, Jenny! I'll no move an inch!'
           Exit Jenny. Neil turns quickly to Davie.
Neil —   'Now for the tricky part! Let's have it,
           Davie!'
           *In a simultaneous move, they exchange bottles,
           tossing them across the stage to each other.*
Johnnie —   'Why, ye pair of rogues!'
Davie —   'Oh, it's all right, Johnnie. If we're no caught,
           we'll pay later!'
Neil —   'What d'ye mean, if we're no caught? She'll
           never guess!'
Johnnie —   'We'll soon see, here's Jenny coming back.'
           Enter Jenny, shaking her head.
Jenny S —   'I'm sorry, Neil. Mistress Angus says it's cash
           or nothing!'
Neil —   'She'll no trust me?'
Jenny S —   'No credit, Neil. That's the rule.'
Neil —   'Well, the miserable ould toe-rag!' *Affecting
           offence*: 'I never thought I'd live to see the
           day that...Och, never mind!'   *Hands the
           bottle to Jenny,*   'Here ye are, lassie — she can
           keep her rotten whisky! It's no worth drinking!'
Jenny S —   'I'm sorry, Neil!'
Neil —   'It's all right, lassie! No blame til ye! If
           Mistress Angus wants cash, cash she'll get!
           It'll be a bit of a trail for me, but I'll off home,
           get the money and stick it doun her miser-
           able throat!'   *To the others,*   'Come on, lads!
           We'd best be on our way!'

As Neil has been talking, Jenny Smith has been examining the bottle.

Jenny S— 'Just a minute, Neil! This bottle....'

Neil— 'What about it?'

Jenny S— 'I think ye'd better take it back.'

Neil— 'Eh? Why should I do that?'

Jenny S— 'I think Mistress Angus is being a wee bittie hard on ye — so I'll cover for ye, if ye like.' *Offers the bottle.:* 'Here, take the bottle even now and bring me the two shillings later!'

Neil— 'Oh, I could hardly do that, lassie!'

Jenny S— 'It's all right, Neil! Here, take the bottle!'

Neil— 'No, no, Jenny! I'll no hear of it! What would happen if ye were discovered? Ye'd lose your place! I'm no having that on my conscience.' *As Jenny S. tries to protest,* 'No, no, lassie — I'll no hear of it, although it's kind of ye to offer. Now, just ye go and put that bottle back on the shelf and I'll be in for it later.'

Jenny S— 'Whatever ye like,' *Conspiratorially,* 'I'll set it by for ye, eh?'

Neil— 'Aye, ye do that, eh?'

Jenny S— 'I'll see ye later on, then. Ye and all, Davie. And... *to Johnnie almost confidentially,* '...I'll be getting a dance with ye the night, Johnnie?'

Johnnie— 'Well, I suppose...'

Neil takes Jenny's arm and hurries her out.

THE CUTTING-OFF PIECE 183

Neil —   'Count on it, lassie! Ye count on it!'

Jenny S — 'Cheerio for now, boys!'
All —   'Cheerio, Jenny! Cheerio!'
           Once Jenny has gone, Neil turns triumphantly
           to the others and gives a cry of exultation.
Neil —   'Oh, Sourrow! What did I tell ye, Davie?
           What did I tell ye?'
Davie —   'It worked all right!'
Neil —   'Like a charm, boy! Like a charm! She swal-
           lowed it hook, line and sinker!'
Davie —   'I thought she had ye there for a minute,
           mind!'
Neil —   'Oh, so did I, boy! So did I! But come on, we
           better get off now — we've a lot to afore the
           night. Ye'll come with us, Johnnie, will ye
           no?'
Johnnie — 'Oh, surely! I'll...'
           Jenny Horne steps forward and waves her arm.
           There is a lighting change and Lizzag Sodger's
           voice is heard, off-stage:
Lizzag —   'By the right, quick march!'
Johnnie — 'What the...'
Neil —   'It's Lizzag Sodger! Come on, Davie — into
           line!'
Davie —   'Right ye are. See ye later, Johnnie!'
           To Johnnie's amazement, Neil and Davie stand
           together at attention as Lizzag Sodger enters,
           marching. She is an old woman who uses a

THE CUTTING-OFF PIECE

broomstick as a rifle and she marches all round the stage.

Lizzag — 'Left-right-left-right-left-right...' *She comes to a halt before Neil and Davie.* 'Halt!' *Considers them.* 'Squad — squad at ease! Stand easy! Let us pray.' *To Johnnie's amazement, Neil and Davie bow their heads in reverence as Lizzag prays.* 'Lord, bless the yaams and the white tatties! Lord, bless the gricie and make him soon intil a muckle soo. Lord, bless Donald and give him long legs to cross the river! Amen.' *Lifts up her eyes, bellows:* 'Squad — squad, attention!' *Neil and Davie come to attention and Lizzag inspects them:* 'Cormack, ye're improperly dressed, man. Improperly dressed!' *Davie buttons his jacket.* 'Gow, what's the matter with ye? Growing a beard, are ye?' *Neil strokes his chin.* 'Get yourself a razor, man!' *She turns away from them, approaches Johnnie and gives him a salute. Uncertainly, he half-returns the greeting and Lizzag snaps to attention,* 'Squad — by the right — wait for it, wait for it! — quick march! Left, right, left, right, left, right...'

Drilled by Lizzag, exit Neil and Davie marching, with Lizzag in the rear. Johnnie watches in amused wonder the lights change slowly, returning to the opening state.

Johnnie — 'What the dickens was that?'

Jenny Horne laughs.

Jenny H—	'Ye tell me, boy! I've never seen anything like it before!'
Johnnie—	'Ye mean, ye didna do that?'
Jenny H—	'Me? No! It's your dream, boy — no mine!'
Johnnie—	'A dream? Is that what's happening to me — I'm having a dream?'
Jenny H—	'What else could it be?' *Searchingly,* 'What did ye think it was?' *Johnnie returns to the bench and sits down wearily.*
Johnnie—	'I don't know — for a whiley there, I thought...'
Jenny H—	'That ye were back home? That I'd made some magic or other and transported ye back til Dalmachair?'
Johnnie—	'Aye! That's it!' *Longingly,* ' It was all so real! First Maggie — then Neil and Davie and...' pause, 'Jenny Smith...'
Jenny H—	'What about Jenny Smith?'
Johnnie—	'Oh, nothing! It's just that...well, when I saw her, she looked different somehow...'
Jenny H—	'Or maybe ye felt different?'
Johnnie—	'Aye.' Thoughtfully. 'Maybe.'
Jenny H—	'And what about the ould wifie, eh? Who's she?'
Johnnie—	'Oh, that's Lizzag Sodger. Her son, Donald, went off til the army and was killed in South Africa.' *Sighs.* 'It turned her head, poor woman!'
Jenny H—	'Well, that can be the way with dreams.'

THE CUTTING-OFF PIECE

Johnnie—	'What?' *Rises, alarmed,* 'Here, that's no what's happening to me, is it? I'm no losing my...'
Jenny H—	'No, no, Johnnie, never worry!' *Explains,* 'It's just that ye must always be careful how ye read your dreams, that ye understand what they're telling ye. Do that and ye'll be fine.'
Johnnie—	'And what about ye? Are ye a dream and all?'
Jenny H—	'I'm the dream-giver. I bring your dreams to life, set them afore ye and let ye see them properly — so that ye can make up your own mind.'
Johnnie—	'Make up my mind about what?'
Jenny H—	'About who ye are. About what ye're doing. About where ye want to go.'
Johnnie—	'Ach, I dinna need dreams for that!' *Moves centrestage angrily.* 'I know where I want til go all right! I want to go home!'
Jenny H—	'Aye, Johnnie — but are ye sure that ye can?' *Exit Jenny Horne. Johnnie is unaware that she has gone.*
Johnnie—	'Oh, if I had the money, I'm certain I could...' *Notices that she has gone.* 'Mistress Horne? Jenny Horne? Where've ye gone? Where are ye?' *Looks everywhere.* 'What's happening...am I?..Oh, My God, I'm seeing things! That's what it must be. The hunger's going to my head, I'm imagining...' *In a sudden*

panic he rushes to the bench and puts his jacket on. 'I'm getting out of here. I'll go and see Mr Green and ask him to help me!' *Picks up his neckerchief,* 'It's a long trail, but...'

We hear Maggie's voice off, singing the song we heard earlier. Johnnie drops the neckerchief and claps his hands to his ears.

Johnnie — 'Stop it! Stop it! Stop it! No more, no more!' *He breaks down, sobbing, first to his knees, then to his fac:* 'No more dreams! No more visions! I want to go home! I want to go home! I want to go home!'

The song comes to an end. Enter Jenny Smith slowly, dressed for the evening. As Johnnie hears her footsteps, he lies quiet, not knowing what might happen.

Jenny S — 'What are ye lying down there for, Johnnie Mackay?'

He looks up and sees her.

Johnnie — 'Jenny!'

Jenny S — 'What's the matter with ye, laddie? Ye'll get yourself into a terrible mess!' *Helps him up and dusts him down.* 'Come on, now — I canna be seen with ye the night in such a state!'

Johnnie — 'Seen with me?'

Dance music, faintly at first, begins to play.

Jenny S — 'Well, ye promised me a dance, did ye no?'

Johnnie — 'What? Oh, no!'

THE CUTTING-OFF PIECE

Jenny S— 'Oh well, then, if ye've changed your mind...'

As Jenny turns to leave, Johnnie impulsively moves to stop her,

Johnnie— 'Jenny, wait!' *Takes a deep breath, calms himself:* 'I've no changed my mind. A promise is a promise, eh?'

The music grows louder. Enter the dancers, all the characters plus extras as required, led by a musician. Jenny and Johnnie join them. When the dance ends, everyone claps and cheers. Neil Gow steps forward.

Neil— 'Well, well, everybody, I think ye'll agree with me that it's been a grand evening!' *Rumble of assent.* 'But all good things must come to an end and...' *Cries of protest which Neil joking dismisses,* 'Good Lord, what's the matter with ye all? Have ye no had enough?' *Cries of 'No' and a general demand for 'The White Cockade'. Neil holds up his hands for quiet.* 'All right! All right! Ladies and Gentlemen, by special request, there will be one last dance — 'The White Cockade!' *Cheers.* 'Lads, give us a hand with the benches. Davie, will ye do the honours?'

Davie— 'Surely, Neil! As long as ye're no wanting a kiss!'

General laughter. The benches are moved centrestage and all the girls sit down on one side and all the men on the other. The musician strikes

THE CUTTING-OFF PIECE   189

a chord and Davie begins the dance by dancing in a circle and dropping a neckerchief at the feet of Maggie Fraser. Maggie picks up the neckerchief, gives Davie a kiss and joins him in another circuit, stopping to drop the neckerchief at the feet of the young man, who picks it up, gives Maggie a kiss etc...The dance proceeds in this way until only Johnnie is seated and Jenny Smith has the neckerchief. She drops it at his feet, but as he stoops to pick it up, the other dancers form a ring round Jenny. Johnnie had the neckerchief but cannot get into the ring.

Jenny S— 'Come on, Johnnie! Come on!'

Johnnie— 'I canna! They'll no let me!'

Exit the dancers and musician, still playing. Johnnie tries to follow but finds he cannot leave.

Jenny (off)— 'Come on, Johnnie! Come on!'

Johnnie— 'I canna, Jenny! They'll no let me! They'll no let me!' *Comes to himself and examines the neckerchief in his hand. Smiles as he realises it is his own.* 'They'll no let me.'

Enter Jenny Horne.

Jenny H— 'So ye found out for yourself, Johnnie Mackay?'

Johnnie— 'Aye, Mistress Horne. That last dream was none of your making.'

Jenny H— 'So now ye know, eh? Ye canna go back.'

Johnnie— 'No. There's no road back — only the road ahead.' *Ties his neckerchief about his neck.* 'I'll

          THE CUTTING-OFF PIECE

bide here in Glasgow and do what I came here to do.'

Jenny H— 'Make your fortune?'

Johnnie— 'Aye! Some way or other — the Lord only knows how!'

Lighting change. Enter the characters of the dream slowly. Maggie laughs mockingly.

Maggie— 'Make your fortune? Dream your fortune, you mean! That's all ye're fit for, Johnnie Mackay! Ye'll dream your life away.'

Johnnie— 'No, Maggie! No more dreams. This time I'll do it properly. I'll show ye — I'll show them all!'

Neil— 'Aye, ye will that, boy! Ye'll do whatever ye set your mind on doing — like we always knew ye would!'

Davie— 'Ye'll be Lord Provost of Glasgow afore ye're done, Johnnie!'

Jenny S— 'Aye, but will ye be happy, Johnnie Mackay? Cut off from your own folk and all?' *Sadly,* 'Now ye've lost us, ye'll forget us altogether!'

Johnnie— 'Oh, Jenny! How could I do that? How could I forget what's inside my own head?' *Turns to Jenny Horne,* 'Besides, I know one thing for certain.'

Jenny H— 'What's that boy?'

Johnnie— 'If my memory goes astray, if I'm ever in danger of forgetting who I am or where I

came from, I'll always have Jenny Horne
close at hand to bring it all back to me!'
Jenny Horne laughs.

Jenny H— 'As Neil Gow would say — count on it, boy!
Ye count on it!'
*With a flourish of her arm, Jenny Horne snaps
her fingers and all the lights go out.*

THE LAST BLACK HOOSE

Robert Alan Jamieson

HERE WAS NO FEELING LIKE IT. Nothing to compare with this feeling of homecoming, of the moment when the steamer would come round the headland at the Knab and reach the shelter of the harbour, of the moment when his feet would be upon the pier. This was his place, this island. *Bon hoga.* The ferry ploughed northwards, courting the shadows of the wintery peat hills around Cunningsburgh and Quarff. He turned away from the rail and went below to fetch his bags from the cabin.

When he reached the purser's office laden down with his cases, a number of fellow passengers had already assembled with their luggage around them, like walls to keep the strangeness of travelling out. The boy sat down on a long red vinyl seat and waited for the engines to slow. That was the sign that the berth was in sight. One or two people he knew were standing nearby but he couldn't be bothered with talking, so he took a book from his bag and pretended

THE LAST BLACK HOOSE

to read. Out the porthole through the salt spray he saw the lightouse at Bressay slip silently past.

The door in the ship's side was open and he pushed forward in the disorderly queue. The tide was high and the boat well above the pier. Through the gap, over the shoulder of the deckhand making ready to take the gangway from below, he saw his father, wandering slightly bent-backed along the pier, looking up at the faces on board.

The boy took hold of his luggage and got in the line of people going ashore. In front of him, a huge fat man with two great cases and another two bags slung over his shoulders kept getting stuck between the narrow sides of the gangway. The steps rattled and swayed as he went down. The damp harbour air was like a wash under a cold tap.

His father stepped forward to meet him, a welcome on his face. It was four months since he'd last been home. Fæder's large calloused hand slapped him on the shoulder.

—Boy, fu is du?

—Aaricht. An you?

The polite form of the pronoun, reserved for social superiors and the plural. His father gestured sameness and moved off towards the van.

—An hoo's da University gyaain, dan?

University. The word was alien here, as this world was alien there. The two tongues in the boy's head struggled for space, seeking after individuation. He didn't answer, but shrugged. Together they walked

THE LAST BLACK HOOSE   197

from the pier to the car park. Opening the back door of the van to put his cases inside, the smell of unwashed wool rose powerfully to meet him. It was the smell of his father's work, shocking and familiar to him at the same time. Rolls of hessian sacks used for packing the wool lay in the middle of the metal floor. He shoved them out of the way, put his bags inside and tried to close the door, but the lock sprang open. His father signalled him out of the way, and shut it with a flourish, as a forklift whined by on its way to unload the steamer.

Inside the van, his father spoke.

— Aald Robbie o' Snusquoy de'ed last nicht. I met da doctor on da wye here.

— Robbie? The boy thought of the house at Snusquoy, the last black hoose in the toonship. The caddy lamb under the stove, the wet peats in the porch, the hens traiking in and out through the open doors. The two sisters, one of them that couldn't talk and the other that wouldn't, at least not unless it was absolutely unavoidable. They said that she just pointed to the things she wanted in the shop.

— We'll hæ t'gying t'da funeral, his father asserted, drumming his fingers on the steering wheel, while he waited for the exit from the car park to clear.

— Ja.

The boy would go. Robbie had been a kind man, despite the family's straightened circumstances, contributing to all the collections, always giving the bairns a shilling or two if he was down from Snusquoy

at the Post Office. He had the respect of the folk, even them that most abhorred the filth they lived in at Snusquoy. The boy could hear him yet, hooting down on the awe-filled peerie faces staring up at the tall ragged figure with the silver in his hand: *Buy yoursels a bit o chocolate. It's good stuff you ken, keeps oot da caald.* Never with a patronising tone like some, or with a warning to be good, but always with the same short inhalation of breath as might precede the sharing of a secret, followed by the almost surreptitious passing of the coin.

Fæder cleared his throat and lit a cigarette.

—Dere'll be gød turnoot, mark du me. He wis weel lækit wis aald Robbie.

The boy felt no shock at this death. He had experienced many, as the community grew older and the houses fell vacant. Crofts were signed over and amalgamated into larger units by the few that had the energy or the vision for a better way of living. But the number of folk was dropping away, and the boy knew that communities could die. That had been the fate of his mother's birthplace, when the car and van replaced the boat as mode of transport. And just the previous year, she had gone with the others, leaving the north end of the house a mausoleum, full of all her things that no one in the family had the heart to throw away.

The van traced a two-tyre pattern on the dewy road to the west. It was early and only the odd car passed on its way to the toon and the work. The boy knew

the bends in the road with his eyes shut. As a child, he had often kept them closed as a test of memory. The sequence of these rolling motions was a sign of return.

It would be difficult telling his father that he wasn't going back to Edinburgh. It would come as a kind of rejection of his mother's will. She had so much prized that education, which she as a girl from a poor crofting family during the war could not aspire to. But the boy knew that he would have to do it. He glanced at his father's face to see if there might be present some clue as to the right approach.

The face was as it had been, for almost as long as he could remember. Heavy pendulous skin hanging from cheekbones lineless, broken only by a soft fleshy mouth and bulbous nose. The eyes bright to the point of becoming opaque. Only the white hair marked it as older, though that was thick as it had ever been and still swept back in a curve established years ago by a hair cream long discarded. The soft mouth opened.

—I wis trying t'tink whit'n an age o man Robbie wis, he frowned. Then grinning, —Fir aa da dirt dey lived in, yon Snusquoy folk ir no døn bad. I mean dær's aald Frankie, he wis seeventy-tree, and Robbie widna been muckle less. An bæth Annie an Jessie ir been draain da pension fir twartree year noo. Hit mak's de tink, døsn it? Dær's some dat'll live in spite o demsels an idders — he hesitated — weel I canna help tinkin o dy pør midder, boy, never drank a drap,

THE LAST BLACK HOOSE

never even smokkit a fag and she never even saa fifty.
Quhile aald Robbie's sookin awa on a bottle o horse
lineament.

—Horse lineament? He drank dat?

—Ach weel so some fok say. Did du never hear o
dat?

Astonished, the boy turned away to gaze out the
side window as the van climbed up the side of the
hill of Weisdale, through pale sunlight now filtering
through the foggy morning. The shapes of the many
tiny islands lying in the mouth of the voe formed a
grey blue abstract puzzle which his memory sought
to complete.

The last miles home passed silently. Just inside the
hill dykes of the toonship, they passed the house at
Snusquoy. The doctor's car was outside. The boy
looked in the but end window and saw the solitary
bare lightbulb, the only speck of contact with the
world of electrical marvels. A black and white sheep-
dog came tearing out from the porch and chased
snarling after the van until it was outpaced.

— Damn føl dog, said Fæder.

The boy looked back to the dog, where it had
stopped in the middle of the road, still directing an
occasional bark after them.

—Dey hæ næ use fir it noo. Hit'll be better aff if
dey hæ it pittin doon.

The van pulled up at the side of their house. It
looked shabbier than it had, even four months before.
The honeysuckle which had wrapped itself around

the porch was gone, lying hunched into a great ball of stem and leaf at the side of the house.

— Whit happened t'dis?

— Ach, it came doon wi da last gæl. I never hed ony time t'see t'it.

They went into the but-end and took their jackets off. Fæder emptied the tea-pot and put a kettle on the rayburn to boil. The boy went to the door, saying he would take his bags to his room up the stair.

Once outside with the door closed, he didn't mount the stair, but hesitated. He opened the north end door. Everything was as it had been, save for an increase in the dust. The photograph of Grobsness still hung above the fireplace, next to the old American clock. On the mantle stood the photo of her as a young woman, a picture that had always intrigued him because in it she still had her own teeth. Furniture, clothes, ornaments, all lay as it had four months before. He stood a moment taking in the sight, then closed the door behind him and went up the stairs with his bag.

Fæder had made the tea when he got back down to the but end. He was listening to the eight o'clock news. They ate from a packet of biscuits while the radio voice told them what the world was like today. Fæder was silent. Maybe he knew the boy had been in for a look.

— I'll hæ t'gying. I've somebody comin wi oo, he said, standing up.

— I'll gie you a haand, the boy offered.

THE LAST BLACK HOOSE

His father fetched him out a pair of overalls from the cupboard and they went out the back door, up the brae to the old byre, now bereft of kye. It was here that Fæder worked, sorting out the wool clips from the crofts and packing them up for shipping to the mainland mills.

The morning had come good. The sun shone clear and bright now. The sea was still and the rush of waves from the nearby beach was soothing. Fæder stopped and looked out over the meadow land. The boy did the same. He knew every undulation of the treeless landscape intimately, could have drawn it from memory as quick as a glimpse.

In the distance a tractor was at work, with two figures perched on the planter, setting tatties. The stillness of the morning allowed the distant sound to echo across the thin coastal strip of arable land.

—Du can hear da bell ringin on da planter, boy, Fæder said as he lit a cigarette, and stood a moment staring into space.

—Aathing's aaricht is it, wi da University. Du's been very quiet aboot it, he asked.

Surprised, the boy couldn't answer immediately. Fæder sensed the problem, it was clear. The boy sighed.

—It's juist dat, weel I'm no sae sure its richt fir me.

—Richt fir de? Surely du means is du richt fir it? Fir du's da wan dat'll hæ t'change, no hit.

—I dønna ken if I can.

Fæder laughed. —Aabody can change, my boy. An maist o wis hæ tæ. Du's næ different in dat.

He stared at him as if he was giving a backward pupil a necessary lesson. The boy blushed.

—Bit dænna let it happen tae de if du's no ready. Da mær times du bends, da mær brittle du gits. Du's young yit. Tak du dy time.

A small blue van approached, and came to a stop outside the byre. The backdoors were tied with a bit of rope and between them the sacks of wool bulged out. A woman got out the driver's door.

—Mimie, is dis de? I wis expectin Lowrie.

—He's no been weel, man, she answered.

—Sam aald trouble?

—Ja ja, juist yon weary back o his.

She walked round to the back doors and began unfastening the rope.

—I see dir settin tatties roond here already, she observed.

Fæder grinned. —Ja. Trang wirkin fok roond here, no læk yon Glimmerwick crood.

Mimie laughed. She turned to the boy. —Sam aald Bobby. Alwis pullin da leg.

They carried the bags one by one into the shed and started weighing, hooking them up onto a balance hanging from a rafter. The smell of the animals was strong. Fæder claimed he knew the breeds by that alone.

He sniffed and spoke.

—Blackface an Cheviot again dis year, Mimie?

She made a face and snorted. —Ja, ja, but du kens, boy, du gits sicna size o lambs.

—Coorse bruck o oo, though.

They agreed an overall weight, to be graded later, and Fæder settled back on the bags of wool to get the news.

—Did du hear, lass, aald Robbie o'Snusquoy's de'ed.

—Aald Robbie?

—Ja. Last nicht it wis.

—Weel, dang me, I never tocht he wis still livin. He most a been a terrible age?

—Seeventy plus, I reckon.

—Is dat richt? An him still livin in yon aald black hoose.

Fæder nodded. —Black aaricht. Da last teckit røf roond here.

—Hed he ony fæmily?

—Twa sisters still itida hoose.

—Nane o dem merried?

—Na, nane o dem ever merried. Guid kens whit'll come o dem noo. En o dem's a dummy, an da idder en, tho she can spæk, says precious little. Hardly gying oot o da hoose, da pair o dem. I canna see dat dey'll lat dem gying on livin yondroo noo dat Robbie's gien.

Fæder went with Mimie to the van. The boy stayed in the byre. When Fæder came back they started

sorting the clip, the boy opening the bags and emptying the contents onto the floor, while his father threw the fleeces onto different piles. They worked silently until the last bag was spilled out. Fæder stooped to pick up a fleece which was rolled up tight like the others, but which was clearly different from its colour and its web.

—Well, weel weel, he muttered. —Wid du look at dat.

He unrolled it and held it up to the beam of light coming through the small sash window. Here and there, peat dust trapped in the fibres gave it a faint reddish tinge. When it was opened out fully the boy saw in it a pattern so naturally perfect that he pictured a piece of lace work. Certain areas of the fleece were clumped into little peaks, while in others the strands of wool were drawn out so thinly as to be virtually transparent. The pattern of these occurrences was beautiful.

—See? Even in da worst clip du sometimes fins wan. Pure Shetland dat. No a drap o cross near it. And turning he laid it carefully in a place by itself, under the window. The boy stared at it for a while. —Beautiful, he said, not thinking.

The work over, Fæder leaned back against the door of the byre.

—Did du ken, dey say dat Shetlan oo is owre fine t'be spun commercially. Dey say dey hæ t'mix some coorser oo in wi it, so da yarn will hadd tagidder. Bit

I'm no sæ sure. I mean, which did da aald fok use if it wisna pure Shetlan, eh?

The boy nodded. —Most hæ been.

—Noo I ken a muckle modern frame is no da sam as a peerie spinnie, bit still if du took da time t'do it richt, eh? I reckon it cood be don.

Fæder stood back from the door. —Gying du if du wants tæ. Hæ a bit o a waandir. I'll be gittin som dennir aboot wan.

The boy walked down over the links to the beach. He was thinking about what his father had said about the wool and about old Robbie, the old man's charitable ways and the darkness of his life in poverty and dirt. Was it possible for the two to be separated out? Was it possible for that pure yarn to be spun on modern equipment, or would the thread just snap and recoil?

The links had been eaten away by the sea over recent years, till the narrow neck of land that separated the freshwater loch from the ocean was no more than a stone's throw in width. He walked around the shoreline till he came to the derelict Haa, where the lairds of old had lived. In the distance he could see the house at Snusquoy. Yes, this was his place. That would always be so. But if he stayed would the spectres of isolation and death hang over it, so that he could not avoid the chilling sense of loneliness he knew so well; but if he left, could he remain himself outwith this place, pure spun, without the necessary coarse addition?

There was a way to find out.

The funeral drew an army of men to the kirk. Cars covered the ground outside the dyke and far back down the road beyond. Figures in dark cloth stepped into the kirk, removing hats and picking up hymnaries. Neither of the sisters were there. They had been moved out of the black hoose, to an old folk's home in the toon.

The minister made much of Robbie's generosity and humility. He read the story of the widow's mite and said that the dead man had given of his labour and himself freely, that he had embodied a spiritual contentment rare in the modern age, regardless of worldly goods. There was no need to make a point of the cleanliness of his soul, in contrast to his environment.

After the service, the fleet of cars drove in convoy through the village at a respectful speed to the place of burial. The Post Office was shut for the duration of the ceremony. The children were kept indoors and all work in the rigs was suspended.

The kirkyard was a half-mile off, yet when the hearse reached its destination, the last of the line of cars had not left the kirk. Fæder and the boy came somewhere in the middle. They stood a little way off from the graveside. During the ritual throwing of earth, the boy caught sight of his father's eyes as they strayed to the stone that bore his mother's name. Their vision momentarily met. When the burial was

THE LAST BLACK HOOSE

done, they moved towards the gate with a new sense of union. Fæder turned to him and spoke.

—She'd hæ been prood, du kens, o de at da University. She used t'say du'd go far.

The boy nodded, a ball of guilty feeling blocking his throat.

—It sood o been her, no me. It wis her dræm, no mine.

—Mebbe, boy, mebbe. So du's no gyaain back?

—No.

—Whit'll du dø?

—I tocht mebbe we cood see if dis spinnin frame wid wirk.

Fæder raised his eyes and sighed, with a smile on his face.

—Mebbe.

As they passed a group of men at the gate, the boy overheard them discussing the great revelation of the day when the district nurse had gone to pack the sisters' gear for them to take away with them. She had found in a kist under the bed, in the traditional place, a small fortune in uncashed pensions and neatly folded notes.

Fæder nodded his head firmly. —Dær's wan thing we hæ t'dø, boy. We most gying ina yon nort room an sort it oot. Will du help me?

The boy nodded.

—Ja.

THE LAST BLACK HOOSE   **209**

BUN,
TRI GEUGAN,
DUILLEAG THAR FICHEAD

ROOTS,
THREE BRANCHES,
TWENTY ONE LEAVES

A o n g h a s
M a c N e a c a i l

 n tìr balbh

seòladh

dean sgàile tìm,
    agus seas mun choinneaimh
ma's fhiòr do dheòn
theid do ghiùlain troimhe

an dé

seilean san fhraoch
a trusadh 's a seinn
o bhlàth gu blàth
air àirigh gun chrìch,
mar gum biodh an saoghal
gun òige na aois

he dumb land

directions

make a veil of time
and stand before it,
if your wish is true
you'll be guided through it

yesterday

bee in heather
gathering, singing
from blossom to blossom
on an endless pasture,
as if the world were
without youth or age

cumail chàirdean

each deighe agus each teine
agus mathan donn a ghlinne ghuirm
agus am buabhal naomh

cuid de dhìamhairean nan dream

bradan a linne
damh a frìth
craobh a coille

cuid de dhòchasan nan dream

agus an sgóth de shoillse dubh
an lagh nach do thagh iad
mar chòta-cuthaich, mar ghainntir

eachdraidh

saighdear agus còt air,
còta baillidh,
còta cìobair,
tha 'n creach dall
do mhiadachd sporain

keeping friends

horse of ice and horse of fire
and the brown bear of the green glen
and the sacred buffalo

some of the peoples' mysteries

salmon from the pool
stag from the moor
tree from the forest

some of the peoples' expectations

and the cloud of black light
the law they did not choose
like a strait-jacket, like a gaol

history

a soldier wearing a coat,
a bailiff's coat,
a shepherd's coat,
plunder is blind to
a purse's measure

aon seach aon

gabh an rathad eadar
na smuaintean, tha iad cho
cas, le chéile, an té
a tha dubh agus an té a tha
buileach, buileach geal

dùthaich

tha do shùil mar thobar, cho glan
's gu bheil a ghrunnd mar mhol tràghad
ri soillse gréine,
gach éideag saillte tioram deàrrsach,
tha eachdraidh tuatha na do bhùirn,
neart ùr dhan taisdealaiche,
ceann-uidhe bradain

dóbhran is duine

ma roinneas sinn
an linne seo
tha bradan dhuts ann
tha bradan dhòmhsa

one or the other

take the road between
the thoughts, they are so
steep, both, the one
that is black and the one that is
altogether absolutely white

country

your eye like a well, so clean
its ground is a shingle beach
in sun's bright heat
each salt pebble dry, dazzling,
there's a people's story in your water,
fresh strength for the traveller,
salmon's destination

otter and man

if we share
this pool, there's
a salmon for you
a salmon for me

ROOTS, BRANCHES, LEAVES　　　　　**217**

alba

dal rìata

do mhachraichean leathann
do mhachraichean arbhair
do sgeòil ann an clach agus
d'ùrnuighean gràinchloiche
àrd agus sìnte

do chòmhraidhean diamhair
le gealach is grian

agus
do sholuis a deàrrsadh
aig samhuinn aig bealltainn
a sealltainn an rathaid

aig crìochan do mhachair, a choille
is farum nan tuagh

scotland

dal riata

your widespread plains
your widespread cornfields
your stories in stone and
your granite prayers
raised and reclining

your secret conversations
with moon and with sun

and
your lamps blazing
at samhuinn and beltane
lighting the road

at the edge of your plains, the forest
and slashing of axes

cul lodair

caoran ruadh
air fàich nam bàs
nam bruadar

ach fhathast 'sa chuimhne
tha claidheamh glan
na chrann 'san fhonn

innleachd
1. *glas cau*

anns a ghlaic ghorm seo
dh'éirich luingeas mar dhuileach
duileach stàilinn a sgaoileadh amach
thar nan cuan

lìon an ghlac le
ceathach stàilinn,
aodainn cho liath ri
aois

culloden

red rowans
on the field of deaths
of dreams

but still in memory
a clean sword
ploughs good earth

invention
1. glas cau / glasgow

in this green hollow
shipping grew like leaves
leaves of steel spreading out
across oceans

the hollow filled with
a fog of steel,
faces as grey as
age

2. cluaidh

eil cuimhne eil cuimhne
cruinn-togail mar chorracha-liath
treud air spiris an t-sruith
a togail nid stàilinn

mar a thog iad air falbh
aon an deidh aon
gun isean a chaoidh

amairigea

damh is sealgair — am machair mór

seall orm 's mi 'g amas mo shaighead
thoir dhomh cliù do léirsinn
's do bhàs na mo run

ma tha m'urram na d'anam ag éirigh
tha mi cinnteach gu'n aithnich do dhream
's gu'n till iad

2. clyde

is there memory, memory
shipyard cranes like gray cormorants
a flock perched by the stream
building nests of steel

how they took off and flew
one by one
not mourning their chicks

america

stag and stalker — the great plains

look at me as I aim my arrow,
give me the respect of your glance
as I shape your death

if my honour rises entwined in your breath
I'll be certain your kind will know it,
that they will return

ùrnuigh

chuir mi saighead dhan speur
cha do mharbh i
iolaire no dia

nuair a ràinig i àirde nan àirde
chaidh i na lasair, a boillsgeadh
thar àrd-bheann thar chuan

thug dannsa 'n t-soillse
am bradan gu bàrr na linne
's an damh gu bàrr chnuic,
nan iongnadh,

ghlac mo dhreamsa aire nan creach
is lìon iad an stòr

monaidhean dubha dakota

ma ghearras tu seice nan cnoc seo
na do shannt airson òr
sgàinidh tu m'anam

prayer

I put an arrow in the air
it neither killed
eagle nor god

when it reached its utmost height
it became a flame, blazing
over high peak and ocean

the dance of light brought
the salmon up to lake surface
the stag astride ridge
in wonder,

my tribe caught the eye of their prey
and took a winter's meat

black hill of dakota

if you cut the skin of those hills
in your greed for gold
you'll pierce my soul

ROOTS, BRANCHES, LEAVES   225

coup

thug mi sgleog do
chlaigeann òg calgach
sàr-churaidh mo nàimhaid
is thill mi gu m' fheachd fhìn
le gàire

thug mi coinnean a doire
is dh'fhàg mi an treud ann
nan seinn is nan dannsa

hokkaido

an latha sèimh ud

cha tàinig na mathain amach as a choille
's a choille mar bhian air na beanntan
a calg gu crìochan na h-aibhne

choisich sinn mol geal na h-aibhne
nis fhìn is tu fhéin, is
am mathan beag bàn, ar pàisde

coup

I gave a skelp to
the young maned head of
my enemy's bravest brave,
returned to my own band
laughing

I took one rabbit from a copse,
let the warren continue
its singing, its dancing

hokkaido

that tranquil day

the bears did not come out of the forest
the forest that lay like a skin on the mountains
its fur to the banks of the river

we walked the river's bleached pebbles
you, and I, and
the little blond bear, our infant

còmhdhail nam bàrd, aig tigh chida-san

ameasg achaidhean buidhe arbhair,
toradh de bhriathran
ag éirigh dhan iarmailt
sgaoth mòr loin-dubh, a seinn

tigh an eadhainn liadh

dealan-dé san t-seann t-sabhal ùr
a dannsa mar
bhlàthan a sgaoileadh
dàn an déidh dàn an dèidh dàn

na lean

fada cian bho'n
chraobh eòlach
cuiridh an duilleag
friamhach eile
san talamh ùr

228   BUN, GEUGAN, DUILLEAG

poet's congress, at the house of chida-san

among yellow fields of corn,
a harvest of words
ascends to the sky,
a great shoal of blackbirds, singing

the gray ivy house

butterfly in the new old barn
dancing like
blossoms scattering
poem after poem after poem

what followed

far, so far from
its familiar tree
the leaf will grow
another root
in the new earth

ROOTS, BRANCHES, LEAVES

beanntan hidaka

tha mathain is luchainn is féidh
a seinn òrain am beatha
'sa chalg ghorm
tha na bradain a streap
tromh àigh nan eas

bheir an duine
ceadas dhan duine

ainu

tromh cheathach, tromh chreag
chun a bhaile-tasgaidh
tigh-tùghaidh is mathan is bradan,
gach nì a bha naomh na chleas
dhan luchd-turuis,
a chànan na fuigheal
a priobadh mar dhuilleag gun shùgh
air oiteagan foghair,
ach aona ghas-feòir
cho gorm ri dòchas

hidaka mountains

bears and mice and deer
sing the songs of their life
in the green fur
salmon climb
through the joy of waterfalls
a man will issue
permits to a man

ainu

through fog, through rock
to the museum town,
thatched houses, bears and salmon,
all that was sacred now sport
for the tourist,
the language like scraps
of glimmering sapless leaves
on autumn gusts,
one blade of grass
stays green as hope

dualchas

san talla fodair seo
air an ùrlar ard seo
ni mi dannsa dhut
(is tu air thurus)
(m'aoidh urramaich)
ni mi dannsa dhut
na mo sheice mathain
is m' anam ann a seice
nathair nimheil

ach na mo sheice fhìn
tha mi dannsa measg nan craobh
taobh na h-aibhne
cruinn mu'n lasair
agus
bradan na mo cheum
no buaidh

heritage

in this hall of straw
on this raised stage
I'll dance for you
(as you're on tour)
(my esteemed guest)
I'll dance for you
my soul in the skin
of a venomous snake

but in my own skin
I dance among the trees
beside the river
circling the flame
and
salmon in my step
or triumph

THE BIG BOAT
Bess
Ross

 IS TWO SONS LAUGHED AT HIM. "What do you know?" they said.

"If you'll know a quarter of what I know, you'll know plenty", he threw back to them as he scoured the pans in the sink.

"No!" the young one challenged, a smile on his mouth and that light in his hazel eyes.

"Oh but yo," he rose to their bait as with slow deliberation he removed every particle from the inside of the pan. He smiled to himself, shook his head as he remembered. At their age he too thought that he could pass his father. Ay, the old fellow. His laugh was quiet and deep as he wiped the outside of the pan with the scouring cloth. He rested his hands on the edge of the sink, stood awhile. Hands that were once swift and sure were now gnarled and disobedient, the veins on the backs standing out like knotted rope.

THE BIG BOAT

Ay, he was thinking, it would take a better man than himself was to catch the old fellow. Not that he ever stopped trying, at every whip he'd try. He minded when his father got the car, he was the first man in the village to get one. Not that he could drive, he couldn't drive, frightened of the thing he was. The driving was left to himself, the boyan. 'You'd best give it to the boyan', the old fellow'd say to this woman or that one, when they came to pay for the fish.

They went far to sell the fish in those days, Oykel, Lairg, Dingwall, all over, and the old fellow beside him, sitting there like a Duke. Most times it was his mother that did the selling, but there were the times when his father was like a bairn, wanting a run in his new car. And if they stopped for any reason, for whatever reason, it was always the same story, did he have petrol in her? Was he sure?

One time they went to Fort William to see Eachann. He was working on the new road. A Sunday it was, the old fellow wasn't strict like that. His mother was the strict one but she came. She was in the back. Every time they went over a bump in the road, and there were plenty, the toolbox jumped from its place at her.

When they reached Fort William and his mother and father were seeing Eachann in the place he stayed in, himself thought he would take a run out to see Jean, who worked in a hotel outside the town.

He was late getting back, they were waiting for him, his mother standing with thon look about her and the old fellow yarning to someone. Once they were in the car his father just looked at him,"Ay, you were at the coorting", he said, and winked at him. His mother never said a word, no nor all the way home.

"Mind your feet," he said to his own young one, as he knelt in front of the fire. He lifted two lumps of coal from the shovelful on the hearth and added them to the flames. From his chair he looked on the bent heads of his sons as they looked through old copies of *The Fishing News*. In the quiet spell the crackle coming from the fire was comforting to him. The old cat at his feet was purring like a train, with the best part of a tin of salmon inside him.

He remembered that night he thought he would take the car to the dance. He was wanting to impress Nellie Tarrel. That time in Fort William Jean told him to be going, so he went. If he asked for it the old fellow wouldn't give it so he thought to wait until the pair of them were in bed. And he waited and he waited and still they sat.

He thought they were never going to make a move and it would move and it would be ta-ta to Nellie when his mother went ben. Not the old fellow though. He was never like to shift. Just sitting there, no saying a word. The clock was ticking but he was certain it wasn't moving. He never thought time could be so slow, slower than you could ever believe sometimes. By the time his father rose himself was near asleep.

"Well, I think I'll just take a look round, to see what's doing." His voice sounded loud to him in the quiet of the house as his father went through. He waited about until he saw that the lamp was out, and he waited a while longer. He made not a sound as he pulled the garage doors open and pushed the Ford clear, he made no sound as he closed the doors. He thought his heart was going to come out through his mouth when he heard the voice at his back.

"Ay, you rolled her out. Well, you can just roll her back". The old fellow was standing in the door of the house in his drawers and stockinged feet. The following Saturday it was the boat he took to the dance, himself and Dan Flint and Grace Mairac and her sister Jessie. Grace was going with Dan Flint then and Jessie had a notion for himself but ach, he wouldn't take her. Thon laugh that she had would near kill you. "Oh, Jeck, I nearly died," she'd screech in his ear over some stupidness or other. No, but he knew who was near dying. He was glad when she went into service in Glasgow.

His daughter was hard on him when she saw that he had been to the shop in his slippers, and the icy wind coming off the North Sea threatening to cut a body in two. She walked from her home in the next village with good things in her basket: speldings from the fish man for his supper, a madeira cake for his tea and that book she was telling him about from the library van, the one called '*The Silver Darlings*'.

"Move yourselves," she'd cry to her brothers as they toasted their stockinged feet at the dying fire, and she'd build it up before she left to collect her children from the school.

She'd buy him warm clothes at Christmas but that couldn't take the chill from him, and instead of fleshing out his spare frame he appeared more shrunken still in the heavy jackets, thick geansaidhs and warm woollen scarves.

When they were paid off from the oil rigs the talk between the brothers was all boats. They would get this one, they could get that one, they didn't know what way to be with so much money about them. Their father never knew there was money like that in it. Then they decided on one that was for sale up in Kinlochbervie. She sounded right, the kind of boat they were looking for. What did he think? He took the paper from the young one and read what it said. He agreed with them, she did indeed sound a good boat. And the money they were asking was right. They could fish anywhere with a boat like that, his sons said. Yes, he agreed, there was still fish in it. So,

THE BIG BOAT

he thought they should go after her? If they wanted it he said, and they went right away.

The big boat needed a crane to lift it from the lorry into the small garden at the front of the house. There was a dampness in his eyes as they looked at the golden chrysanthemums crushed below its keel.

They never broke stride, hardly took time for a breath. There was work to be done on her and the nights were closing fast. From daybreak until dark they crouched in the bowels of the boat with aching ankles and never put their heads above the gunwhale. And as the first snow flurries of winter grew into a full-throated gale, they froze there. He'd stand in the doorway and call to them that their food was ready and they'd come, climbing over the side like old men.

They'd sit at the table in their working jackets, their faces bent to their plates, as with numbed hands they'd spoon and fork food into their mouths. In silence they ate, grateful for the warmth the food generated. And when it appeared that they would remain about this warmth the older one would draw himself from the table and look to his younger brother.

"Best get back," he'd say.

From the side of the boat he'd reach up a mug of tea to each of them. With thanks softening his face one would descend the planks and pass it to his brother. They swallowed the life giving tea and left their mugs on deck. And in the evening they'd talk

to him. She was needing more work than they thought, costing more than they thought. And in their despondency they'd wonder if they'd got things right or completely wrong. And he who'd known boats all his life would tell them. She was a fine boat and she was worth every penny. They had the time and they had the money, so what was there to sing about. And he told them again about *The Bonnie Lass*, their grandfather's boat.

He had *The Helen* after that, but it was *The Bonnie Lass* he was talking about. Himself and Dan Flint and Hughie Vorrer were the crew. Strong as a bull Hughie Vorrer was, a big strong man.

One day the old man decided he would shoot the lines off the Black Rocks. They should have never left the shelter of the harbour. It was madness that drove them out that day. The sea was boiling, big huge lumps of water coming at them. More than once they thought they had it. All except the old fellow. If he thought they were gone he never showed it. There he stood at the rudder, like a rock he was, never moved, eyes before him and then behind him, taking every wave head on. And when the lights of Wood's farmhouse appeared and they could all breathe once more, he tugged his bonnet over his right eye, his

THE BIG BOAT

way of saying that danger was past, and handed to his son the wheel.

"Take her home, Jakey. Easy now." The old man was the best seaman to come from these parts, knew the sea like the back of his own hand, understood its many moods. And after a rich harvest he used to say, "Ay, she's kind. She gives us everything we need, but she takes too. She always takes, always will."

Many feared them gone that day, the only time he saw his mother crying. Himself was only a boy then and he thought her daft to be dabbing her apron to her face like that.

"Go in", they said as winter tightened its hold and he came out to see how they were progressing. Their tone had a clipped edge to it, masking their deep concern over his frailty.

Wood came from the carpenter, light oak for the new wheelhouse. And as the drifts lay against the fences and the old ones were careful where they walked and the little ones wore their coats and scarves, the hammering and sawing went on. In any dry days they painted the big boat. They gave her a white keel and a blue belly. And in letters of black

against the gunwhale they carefully wrote for him
'The Bonnie Lass'.

His daughter took two pillows from her bed and
placed them beneath his head. She poured porridge
into his plate and he pushed it away, untouched. And
as the full fury of that winter gave the country the
big snow, four old ones went from the village and
quietly he followed. The village moaned to itself and
clutched its breast, dull in its shock. The sea rattled
in its chains and was still.

Dan Flint was still straight at eighty, but as he
walked to his house that day his tread was that of an
old man. For the first time in his life he locked his
door against his neighbour. In the winter greyness,
with his coat still on, he sat by his untended fire and
thought of his friend."Take her home. Easy now".
The words would not leave him.

As the big snow melted and the earth began to
come again, so too did the people of the village begin
to recover from the blow that had been dealt. The old
ones drew their chairs nearer to the flames and tried
to keep their backs warm, and they talked. About
Veelie who was the first to go, and him adamant
always that he had no intention of going before The
Wheeler. Well, The Wheeler was still lifting his pension. All were agreed that the fellow from the Free
Church was no preacher whatever else he was.
No-one could make out a word he said. And what
about that new young fellow from the Kirk. A revelation, he said just what themselves were thinking.
Many a minister twice his age hadn't a command like

THE BIG BOAT

thon. And him with the white trainers beneath the black trousers. But mind, he could speak. They were glad that Jake had him. They could just hear what he would be saying to the other fellow. Ah, and wasn't Jake's box beautiful. Beautiful just. What kind of wood would you say that was? Oh, light oak.

THE RED COFFIN

Iain Crichton Smith

OMETIMES SHE BELIEVED THAT her son was simply lying, at other times she was not so sure. He didn't look like a liar, there was nothing furtive about him when he was telling his stories, but he did seem to dream a great deal. It was as if he wasn't quite of the common earth. Perhaps that was why he was called the Lark by the other boys; they had seized on this unworldliness and his flights of fancy. His latest story however was rather odd. He had come in and asked her casually whether there had been a funeral that day.

"No", she said, though her own dress looked funereal enough.

"That's funny," he said.

"Why should it be funny," she asked. Her hands were white with the flour she had been using for baking.

THE RED COFFIN

"Nothing," he said.

"There is," she said, "or you wouldn't have asked." Was this another lie, another flight? These lies, if they were lies, worried her for she had been brought up to tell the direct truth.

Sometimes however he didn't want to tell her and she had to force what she thought was the truth out of him. Already it seemed as if he regretted his question. But she wouldn't rest.

"Well, what is it then? Why do you think there might have been a funeral?" She would get to the bottom of this, she wouldn't leave it alone.

"It was just..." he said,

"Just what?"

"I thought I saw... what looked like a funeral. Only it couldn't have been a funeral."

"Why not?"

"They weren't wearing black."

"Who?"

"The people."

"What people?"

"The people carrying the... "

"Coffin, you mean."

There was a pause.

"Do they always wear black, mother?"

"Of course they always wear black," she said. "What would you expect them to wear?"

"Yes, only they..."

"Only they what?"

"They were wearing sort of tunics."

"Tunics?"

"Yes, like... You see them in books. They were red and green. And they were wearing pointed hats. Yellow."

"What are you talking about?"

"That's what they were wearing," he insisted stubbornly.

"Who?"

"The people at the funeral. And the... coffin was red."

"What on earth? Where did you see this?"

"At the brae. They were close as... just next to me. They never looked."

"It was your imagination. Who ever heard of a red coffin? And people wearing pointed hats at funerals. It's all these books you read. You must have seen it in a book."

"They were just next to me. I knew one of them."

"Who?"

"I knew Calum Mor. And I think it was Angusan."

"What a liar you are," she said.

"I'm not, I'm not," he screamed.

"Or you dreamed it then. Perhaps you fell asleep and dreamed it."

"I didn't dream it."

But she was relentless.

"Well, then it couldn't have been a funeral. It must have been something else. Maybe you saw a circus". And she laughed.

"There was a coffin," he said. "And it was red. And they were all wearing these clothes."

"A red coffin," she said. "Who ever heard of a red coffin?"

"I saw it," he said. "I did see it."

She looked deep into his eyes which were candid and clear. Something strange stirred within her. Something uncomfortable, eerie. Her own child appeared strange to her. Perhaps he had the second sight. But even if he had, who had ever heard of a red coffin?

She looked down at her hands which were white with flour. This puzzling boy who always seemed to be dreaming.

She tried to imagine a red coffin and couldn't.

"There was something else," he said.

"What was that," she said absentmindedly.

"There was a picture on the coffin."

What was this? A Catholic funeral. Was that what he had seen?

"Of the man in the coffin, maybe. He was wearing the same kind of clothes as the others. He was winking at me. He looked like..."

"Like who?"

"Like Calum Macrae."

"It couldn't be Calum Macrae. Calum Macrae was an elder of the church. He would never wink at anyone, never. He was a big heavy man and looked solemn and important... No, it couldn't have been Calum Macrae."

This was really the height of nonsense. Why should she be listening to this?

"Hadn't you better go and bring in some peats," she said.

"Right," he said. He was always very obedient. After a while he came in with the pail and stood in the door again, the sun behind him. And suddenly she saw it, that extraordinary picture. He was wearing a tunic, red and blue, perpendicular colours. And on his head was a pointed hat. And he was laughing hilariously. She made as if to walk towards him in her black dress but he kept moving on and she followed him out into the sunlight. There he was, a good distance from her, and he was waving to her and she was following him. It was so strange, she seemed to be dancing, and he was dancing as well. And there were flowers all round them, red and white and yellow. How extraordinary.

And in his hand he was carrying a little red box, a beautiful red box like a jewellery box which she had once seen and never had.

And the sun poured down reflecting back from the box while he danced away with it. And she felt so happy, never, never had she felt so happy.

And when she looked down at her dress, it was no

THE RED COFFIN

longer black but green. And his eyes were candid like water. And in them she saw a picture of herself. And the two of them danced onwards together.